ORGY PLUS MASSACRE

SEXY, SCARY & SENSATIONAL CINEMA
1950-1979

VOLUME 3 (1960-1962)

CREDITS

ORGY + MASSACRE V.3
ISBN 978-1-917285-62-9
Edited by G.H. Janus
Text and images copyright © Black Gas Entertainment 2025
https://black-gas.org
Published by Black Gas Books 2025
In association with The Nocturne Group
All world rights reserved
Design template copyright © Broken Fang Cryptography
Published under licence from Fabbrica Sodoma Productions

CONTENTS

FOREWORD	005
HORROR	007
MAYHEM	055
MYTH	097
SCI-FI	127
SEX	155
INDEX	179

FOREWORD

After working with the Nocturne Group on two anthologies of material selected from their ongoing series of books on early cinema,[1] I was delighted when they offered me the chance to edit a new set of film books using photographs and previously unpublished texts from their post-1949 archive. This mass of material was originally to be developed for inclusion in their original series, but was set aside when it became clear that to produce books equally in-depth for the years 1950 onwards would take decades. Instead, I now have the opportunity to include a selection of these basic but still informative texts to enhance this collection of rare production stills.

As such, the ORGY PLUS MASSACRE series will present a visually-led sampling of sexy, scary and sensational cinema from the years 1950 to 1979, three of the most consequential decades in film history. It was during these years that global cinema came of age, not only in the technological sense but especially by way of pushing back the old restrictions of censorship, so much so that by the end of the 1960s, explicit sex and graphic violence had both become accepted in the mainstream. This new liberalism peaked in the mid-70s, when pretty much anything could be legally seen on commercially available film in one form in another, from picture houses to backstreet projection booths. Of course, this provoked an inevitable backlash in the 1980s, but ORGY PLUS MASSACRE will focus purely on these years when film-makers were free to express their most expansive, excessive and extreme visions on celluloid.

Volume 3 includes more than 150 rare and unusual photographs, with accompanying texts, from the years 1960 to 1962. The book is divided into five sections: Horror, Mayhem (delinquency, crime, murder, atrocity), Myth (fantasies of the near and distant past), Science Fiction, and last but not least, Sex (nudity, sexploitation, pornography[2]). When a film falls into more than one category, as many do, the most dominant theme was chosen.

I now look forward to working on the next volumes of this series, with each one revealing how cinema grew sexier, scarier and more sensational with every passing year.

–G.H. Janus

1. The series from the Nocturne Group is entitled SHADOWS IN A PHANTOM EYE, and documents the years 1872 to 1949. I have edited two anthologies of material taken from the series, SATANIC SHADOWS and BEASTS AND BEAUTIES. These represent just a fraction of the content that the series, which runs to 15 volumes and well over 3,000 pages, has to offer.

2. Yes, even in the 1950s and early 1960s loops of pornographic film were available, screened in the most clandestine venues or sold under counters, a situation which continued until Denmark led the legalization of such material from 1968-69 onwards.

L'AMANTE DEL VAMPIRO
("The Vampire's Lover")
Production: Italy, 1960
Director: Renato Polselli
English release title: **The Vampire And The Ballerina**
Category: Horror

HORROR

THE BRIDES OF DRACULA
Production: UK, 1960
Director: Terence Fisher
Category: Horror

A Hammer classic. David Peel plays blond, mummy's-boy vampire Baron Meinster in this arch "sequel" to **Dracula**, somehow reminiscent of Count Stenbock's classic tale *The True Story Of A Vampire*. Christopher Lee was reluctant to portray Dracula again in a hurry for fear of type-casting, leaving Hammer with a dilemma in their desire for a follow-up to their hugely successful initial outing. In the end, **The Brides Of Dracula** retained the services of Peter Cushing as Van Helsing, but Hammer were forced to substitute David Peel as the chief vampire, Baron Meinster; Dracula does not in fact appear. Peel however made an interesting contrast to Lee; blond rather than swarthy, and somewhat sickly and effeminate compared to Lee's aggressive characterisation. Indeed, Meinster is kept locked up in his castle by his domineering mother (Marita Hunt), who prefers to select for herself the female victims to satisfy his vampiric urges. He also has his own nurse (Freda Jackson), a crazed and evil crone who coaxes the dead victims back to life from their graves at midnight. Meinster eventually burns to death in an old windmill whose sails have cast a paralysing cruciform shade upon the ground. The unusually well-etched female characters, emphasising the feminine mood of the film, and Terence Fisher's by now familiar use of sumptuous, saturated Technicolour, helped to make **The Brides Of Dracula** into one of the most attractive and admired films in the whole Hammer *oeuvre*.

CIRCUS OF HORRORS
Production: UK, 1960
Director: Sidney Hayers
Category: Horror

One of several British films made at around the same time which all dealt to varying degrees with mutilation, murder and voyeurism. Hayers' film is the most specifically concerned with surgical cruelty. Dr Schuller (Diffring), a demented plastic surgeon, is on the run after being implicated in the torture of a patient/lover. Posing as a circus-owner, he finds the ideal cover for his practices, peopling his show with the ugliest people he can find, whom he re-models and presents in his Temple Of Beauty. Then, one by one, they try to leave him and soon meet with fatal accidents beneath the Big Top. The sensational murders, coupled with the freak arena of the circus, convey much of the public's voyeuristic appetites; while Schuller's scenes with his patients – lovingly caressing scar tissue, twisted flesh or bloody bandages – have a genuinely perverse quality. An excellent story and subject matter, somewhat ruined by Hayers' pedestrian treatment.

CITY OF THE DEAD
Production: UK, 1960
Director: John Moxey
US release title: **Horror Hotel**
Category: Horror
A superb tale of modern-day witch cults, with future Amicus Films founders Milton Subotsky and Max J. Rosenberg among the producers. Christopher Lee stars as the cult leader.

EL DESPOJO
("The Dispossession")
Production: Mexico, 1960
Director: Antonio Reynoso
Category: Horror

A short film based on the Ambrose Bierce story "An Occurrence At Owl Creek", in which the protagonist imagines whole episodes of experience during the split-second of his death. This is a pessimistic version, enlivened by erotic visions and weird desert apparitions.

DOCTOR BLOOD'S COFFIN
Production: UK, 1960
Director: Sidney J. Furie
Category: Horror
Demented blend of the zombie and Frankenstein myths, with a madman living underground in disused Cornish tin mines where he both reanimates corpses both natural and man-made. Diector Furie also made **The Snake Woman** (1961), in which a doctor's experimentation with venom leads to his daughter developing extremely nasty side effects, such as shedding her skin and fanging the flesh of others. **The Snake Woman** is a 70-minute black-and-white low-budget take on a serpentine shape-shifting theme which would find its most lurid exppression in Hammer's later **The Reptile**.

EL ESQUELETO DE LA SEÑORA MORALES
("The Skeleton Of Mrs. Morales")
Production: Mexico, 1960
Director: Rogelio A. González
Category: Horror/Murder
Supposedly based on Arthur Machen's 1927 story "The Islington Mystery", which in turn was inspired by the Crippen case, this tale of a wife-killer – a taxidermist, like Norman Bates – crosses into horror territory with its final twist. Not content with merely murdering his crippled spouse, the man skeletonizes her corpse and hangs her defleshed bones in his shop window for the world to see.

ET MOURIR DE PLAISIR
("And To Die From Pleasure")
Production: France, 1960
Director: Roger Vadim
Category: Horror
Lush lesbian vampire fantasy, one of many based on Le Fanu's classic story *Carmilla*; this one is probably the most stylish of them all. Oneiric and overwrought, it carries an impressive erotic charge.

HANAYOME KYUKETSUMA
("Blood-Sucking Bride")
Production: Japan, 1960
Director: Kyotaro Namiki
Category: Horror

HOUSE OF USHER
Production: USA, 1960
Director: Roger Corman
Category: Horror
The film adaptation which began Corman's incredibly successful run of Edgar Allan Poe adaptations, featuring regular series lead actor Vincent Price as the neurasthenic Roderick Usher.

JIGOKU
("Hell")
Production: Japan, 1960
Director: Nobuo Nakagawa
Category: Horror

KAIDAN KASANE GA-FUCHI
("Ghost Story Of Kasane Depths")
Production: Japan, 1960
Director: Kimiyoshi Yasuda
Category: Horror

THE LEECH WOMAN
Production: USA, 1960
Director: Edward Dein
Category: Horror/Science Fiction

LA LLORONA
("The Weeping Woman")
Production: Mexico, 1960
Director: René Cardona
Category: Horror
A new version of the horror legend first filmed in 1933, concerning the evil female spirit which haunts a cursed family. This was followed by Rafael Baledón's **La Maldición De La Llorona** (1961, released in 1963).

LA MASCHERA DEL DEMONIO
("The Mask Of The Demon")
Production: Italy, 1960
Director: Mario Bava
English release title: **Black Sunday**
Category: Horror

IL MULINO DELLE DONNE DI PIETRO
("The Mill Of The Stone Women")
Production: Italy, 1960
Director: Giorgio Ferrone
Category: Horror

SEDDOK, L'EREDE DI SATANA
("Seddok, Spawn Of Satan")
Production: Italy, 1960
Director: Anton Giulio Majano
US release title: **Atom Age Vampire**
Category: Horror

Seddok is vintage Italian horror trash, with experiments on horribly scarred Hiroshima victims and a mutant doctor. An insane meshing of surgical horror and killer ape psychodrama, with cinematography by Mario Bava. This US version is severely truncated, and should be avoided.

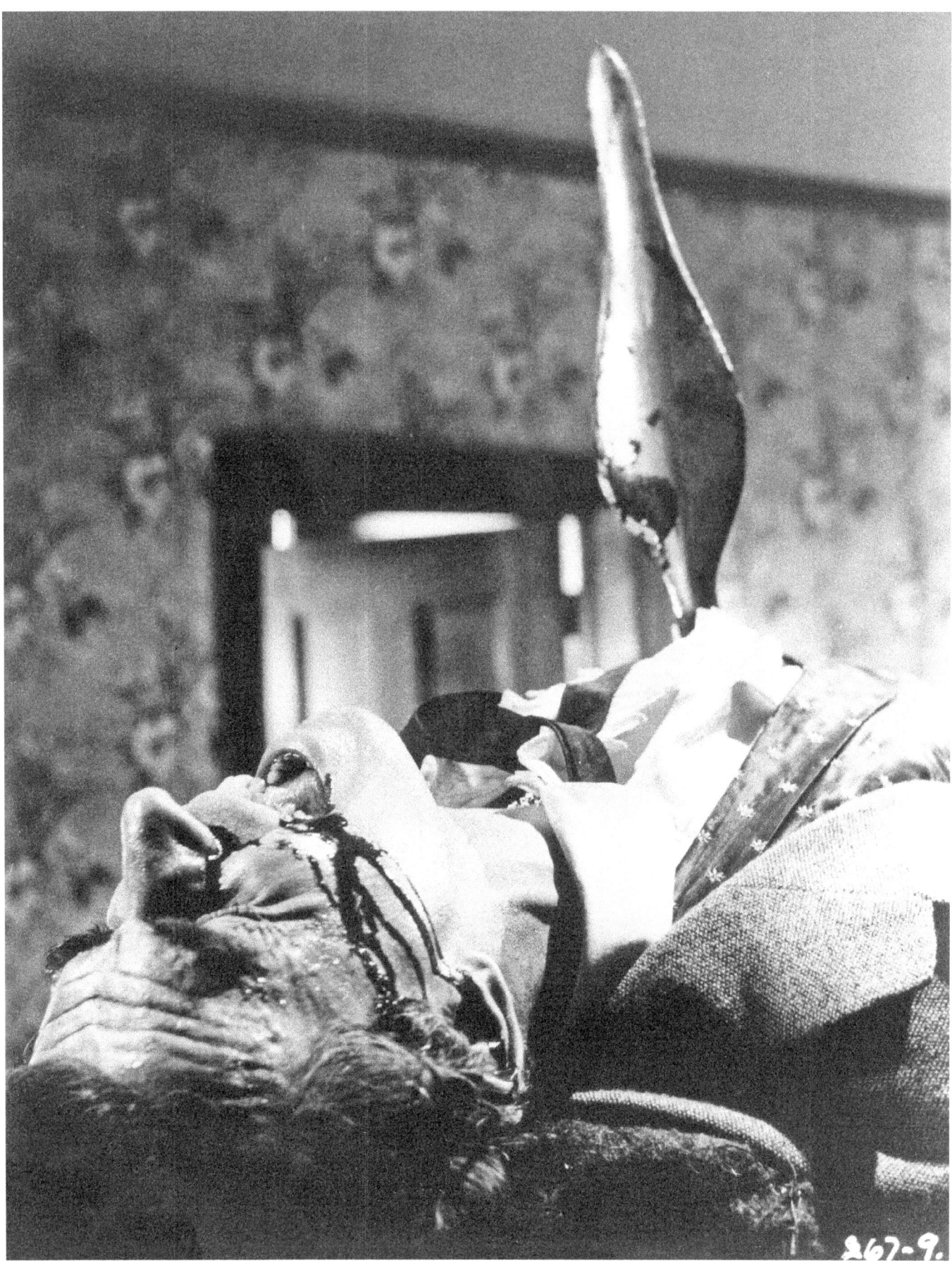

TELL-TALE HEART
Production: UK, 1960
Director: Ernest Morros
Category: Horror

13 GHOSTS
Production: USA, 1960
Director: William Castle
Category: Horror
Castle's entry into the world of cinematic ghosts is set in a house where a family must reside in order to claim an inheritance; unfortunately for them, the house is haunted by thirteen resident spectres who guard the dead man's money. Castle liked to attach a gimmick to each of his films, and in this case it was a process called Illusion-O, which enabled audiences to either see or erase the ghosts from vision, according to which lens of a special "Ghost Viewer" they peered through. Less serious and disturbing as films like **The Haunting**, and not even as scary as his own **House On Haunted Hill** (elevated by the presence of Vincent Price), **13 Ghosts** remains a notable "fun" part of Castle's filmography, linking the "old dark house" films of the 30s with later ghost-shows like Tobe Hooper's (inferior) **Poltergeist**.

TORMENTED
Production: USA, 1960
Director: Bert I. Gordon
Category: Horror
YES

EIN TOTER HING IM NETZ
("A Corpse Hangs In The Web")
Production: Germany, 1960
Director: Fritz Böttger
English release title: **Horrors Of Spider Island**
Category: Horror/Science Fiction/Sexploitation

THE TWO FACES OF DR. JEKYLL
Production: UK, 1960
Director: Terence Fisher
Category: Horror/Science Fiction

The Two Faces Of Dr. Jekyll was Hammer's first (and somewhat tedious) of two serious treatments of the Robert Louis Stevenson classic. Writer Wolf Mankowitz gave the plot a new and ingenious twist, making Hyde a clean-shaven, debonair, coolly sadistic figure as opposed to the ravening, bestial character of earlier films (an idea continued by Jerry Lewis in **The Nutty Professor**). Dr. Jekyll (Paul Massie) by contrast is a bearded, sombre scientist who changes his personality out of scientific curiosity and thereby discovers a useful method of avenging his wife's infidelity with his best friend (Christopher Lee once again). Having successfully killed them both, he is unable to resist more murders. Lee had a chance to play the Jekyll and Hyde role in the later **I, Monster** (Amicus, 1971), in which his performance as Hyde was electrifying. Hammer's next, far more entertaining attempt at the story was the brilliant pulp gothic, **Dr. Jekyll And Sister Hyde**.

L'ULTIMA PREDA DEL VAMPIRO
("The Vampire's Last Victim")
Production: Italy, 1960
Director: Piero Regnoli
English release title: **The Playgirls And The Vampire**
Category: Horror
Five gorgeous showgirls take shelter from a storm in an old castle, only to find out that the master of the place is a vampire (played by Walter Brandi).

LA CABEZA VIVIENTE
("The Living Head")
Production: Mexico, 1961
Director: Chano Urueta
Category: Horror

Mexican variation on the stock mummy theme, in which the head of a dead Aztec leader is awoken by tomb-raiders and seeks awful retribution.

CURSE OF THE WEREWOLF
Production: UK, 1961
Director: Terence Fisher
Category: Horror

Oliver Reed's stand-out Hammer role/performance as Leon, unholy progeny of a lunatic and a raped serving-wench born on Christmas Day, and thus cursed with lycanthropy. **The Curse Of The Werewolf,** based on Guy Endore's classic horror novel *The Werewolf Of Paris*, gave director Fisher an ideal chance to explore his predominant preoccupation: the dualistic nature of mankind and his universe. As the werewolf, Reed is superb throughout, and from its very start, with the horrific violation of a young girl by a filthy, syphilitic beggar, the film – Hammer's first (and surprisingly only) treatment of lycanthropy – is a textbook exposition of werewolf lore. Young Leon reveals traces of his true nature even at his christening, when he inadvertently causes the holy font to boil over, and in adolescence takes to wandering by night leaving a trail of mutilated animals in his wake. In adulthood we see him turning into a ravening wolf at each full moon, killing several people until the love of a good woman enables him to suppress his bestial nature. When their relationship is interrupted, he transforms once more and is finally dispatched by a silver bullet. Fisher again takes the chance to experiment with religious symbolism, while expanding the opposition within Leon to explore a host of antagonistic relationships and elements, suggesting constant cosmic and psychic conflict; the film's construction is appositely symmetrical. The result is a layered, unusually adult film; a vivid, brooding testament to primal sexuality, this is maybe still the best werewolf film – although direct comparisons to the only near contender, Joe Dante's **The Howling,** are redundant. Filmed on sets built for the abortive project **The Rape Of Sabena,** a Spanish Inquisition torture-fest which the British censor warned they would ban outright if completed.

THE DEVIL'S MESSENGER
Production: USA, 1961
Director: Herbert L. Strock, Curt Siodmak
Category: Horror

A film assembled from three episodes of a Swedish TV horror series, **13 Demon Street** (directed by Siodmak) and framed by new footage (directed by Strock) of Lon Chaney Jr. as Satan and Karen Kadler as his female harbinger, Satanya (a suicide). She finally delivers to mankind the formula for a massive doomsday bomb, and the film ends with an apocalyptic explosion. This is all actually more entertaining than the three stories, which concern a murdering photographer haunted by the image of his victim, a woman frozen alive for millennia, and a man who meets his destiny in a derelict ruin at midnight.

ESPIRITISMO
("Spiritism")
Production: Mexico, 1961
Director: Benito Alazraki
Category: Horror

A loose version of the classic horror tale "The Monkey's Paw" (which is here replaced by a severed human hand), with the presence of Satan added to make the whole thing even more downbeat. Dealings with the Devil – who was inadvertently summoned by dabbling with a ouija board – have devastated a whole family, and **Espiritismo** shows the grim aftermath. Much slower and less trashy than most Mexican horror films of its period. *The Monkey's Paw* was filmed under that title numerous times from 1915 onwards, and also used as the basis (uncredited) for several other films, such as **Deathdream** in 1972.

THE INNOCENTS
Production: UK, 1961
Director: Jack Clayton
Category: Horror

Based on Henry James' arid ghost novel *The Turn Of The Screw*, **The Innocents** was a surprisingly effective interpretation by Clayton, who had previously directed **The Bespoke Overcoat** (1956), a 33-minute ghost story adapted from Gogol. It would take Michael Winner to unleash the latent erotic potential of James' original novel with his "prequel", **The Nightcomers,** in 1972.

LYCANTHROPUS
Production: Italy, 1961
Director: Paolo Heusch
Category: Horror

The first ever Italian werewolf movie, in which a girl's convent school is stalked by a feral killer. With more savagery and cleavage than comparable films (such as the UK cut of Hammer's **Curse Of The Werewolf**). Female star Barbara Lass (born Kwiatkowska) was once married to Roman Polanski. The film was sadly dubbed, cut and released as **Werewolf In A Girls' Dormitory** for the American market. (Paolo Heusch was certainly no "trash" director – an accomplished cinematographer, his next film was the brutal neo-realist street-gang drama **Una Vita Violenta,** co-written by Pier Paolo Pasolini.)

LA MALDICIÓN DE NOSTRADAMUS
("The Curse Of Nostradamus")
Production: Mexico, 1961
Director: Federico Curiel
Category: Horror

The first of four films edited from a 1959 serial, starring Germán Robles as the vampire son of the prophet Nostradamus, who swears vengeance on those who persecuted and killed his father. The other films were **Nostradamus Y El Destructor De Monstruos**; **Nostradamus El Genio De La Tineieblas**; and **La Sangre De Nostradamus**.

THE MASK
Production: Canada, 1961
Director: Julian Roffman
Category: Horror

Notable for being shot in 3-D, an effect designed to enhance the nightmare sequences experienced by the film's protagonist, a psychiatrist, when he wears an ancient and seemingly cursed tribal mask. The anaglyphic hallucinations were created by Slavko Vorkapich, the master of film montage sequences.

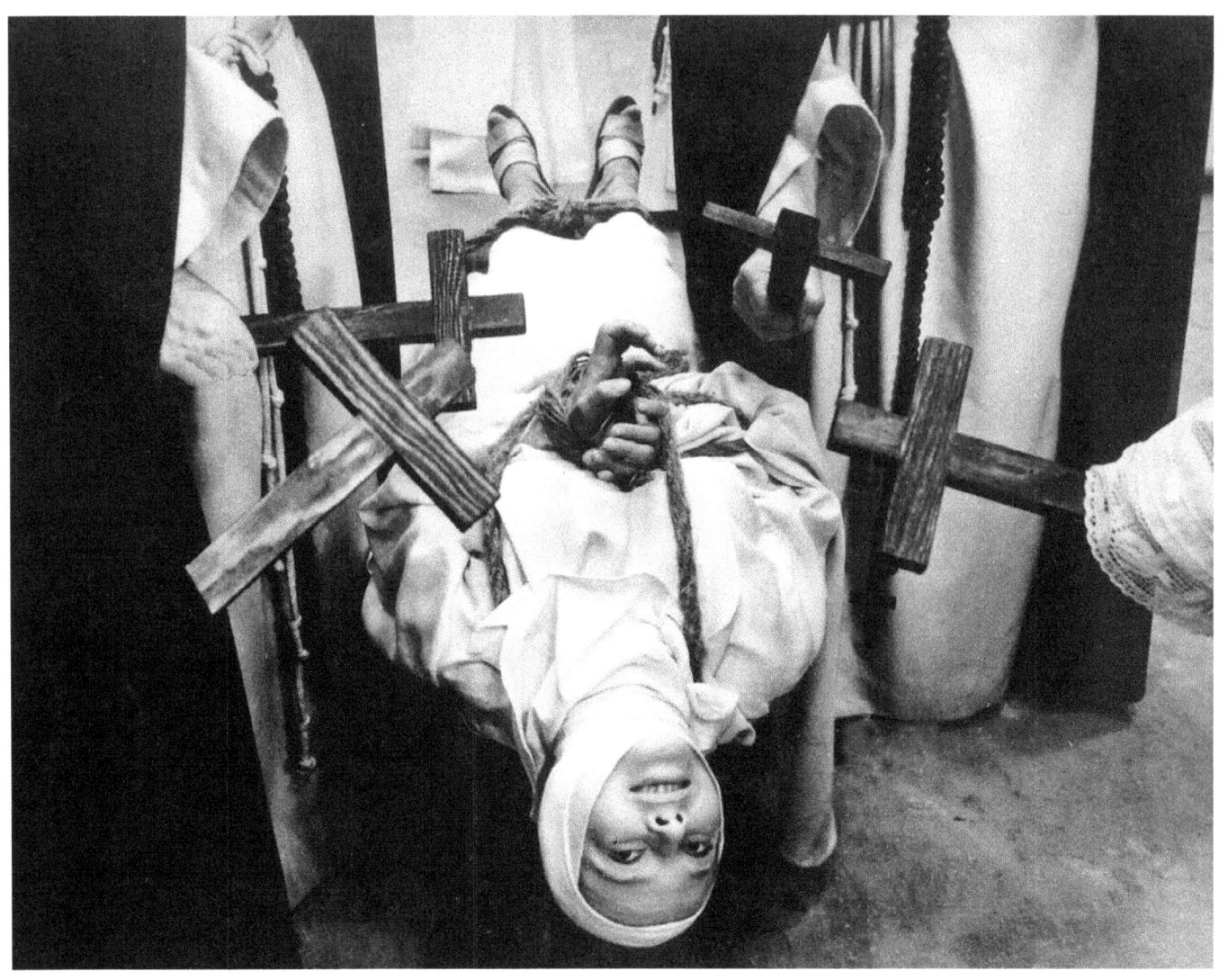

MATKA JOANNA OD ANIOLÓW
("Mother Joanna Of The Angels")
Production: Poland, 1961
Director: Jerzy Kawalerowicz
Category: Demonic Possession
One of the first films concerning "demonic possession" in nuns, with all the covert elements of repressed sexuality, sadomaschism and guilt implicit in the subject matter. A first film treatment of the story of Urbain Grandier, a story which would later be depicted in the most excessive way possible in Ken Russell's **The Devils** (1971). Based upon a novel by leading Polish author Jaroslaw Iwaszkiewicz.

MR. SARDONICUS
Production: USA, 1961
Director: William Castle
Category: Horror
A rare outing into gothic horror from Castle, reprising elements of **The Man Who Laughs** in this tale of a sadist whose face is frozen into a permanent rictus, and the cruelties he perpetrates in his secluded European castle. The odd film out in Castle's run of modern urban frightmares.

EL MUNDO DE LOS VAMPIROS
("World Of The Vampires")
Production: Mexico, 1961
Director: Alfonso Corona Blake
Category: Horror
A gothic vampire movie from the golden age of Mexican horror, crammed full of bats, skeletons, corpses, cemeteries, retarded hunchbacks, thunderstorms, and all the other prerequisites. The one original touch is an organ made of human skulls and bones which the vampire, Count Subotai, plays in his subterranean lair and which has the power to control, kill or enslave other vampires (of which he has a large, zombie-like retinue).

MUNECOS INFERNALES
("Infernal Dolls")
Production: Mexico, 1961
Director: Benito Alazraki
US release title: **Curse Of The Doll People**
Category: Horror
"A Psychedelic Trip Into The Fifth Dimension!" Mexico has produced some of the most grotesque horror movies, and this is a notable example, with dwarfs in fright masks portraying killer voodoo dolls. A shuddering shamble into the twisted teradome of gloating freak horror.

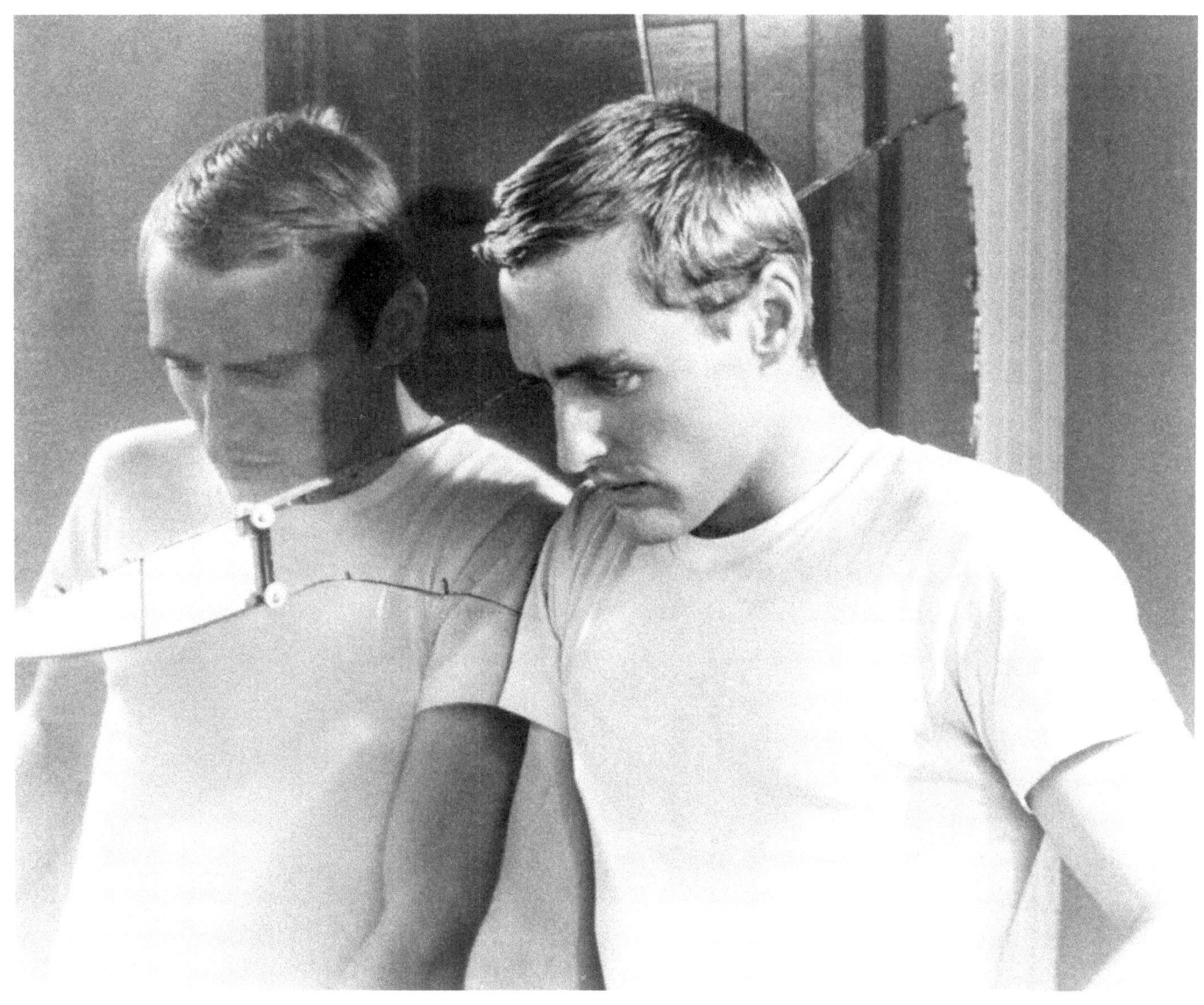

NIGHT TIDE
Production: USA, 1961
Director: Curtis Harrington
Category: Horror Fantasy

A strange fantasy starring Dennis Hopper as the sailor on leave in a Californian coastal resort who comes to frequent a sideshow, where he becomes obsessed with the young girl who plays a mermaid. It turns out that the girl (Luana Anders) truly believes herself to be descended from a race of sea-people, and that she must kill during the full moon as the result of an ancient pelagic curse. The sailor finally finds her dead, drowned in her tank. Recalling Val Lewton's **Cat People** in mood and tone, **Night Tide** is an enigmatic piece which effectively utilises its carnival and littoral setting to establish an other-worldly, fatalistic tension. A genuine occult edge is added by the inclusion of actress Marjorie Cameron, former consort of Crowleyan magician Jack Parsons and one of the dark stars to be glimpsed in Anger's **Inauguratiuon Of The Pleasure Dome**.

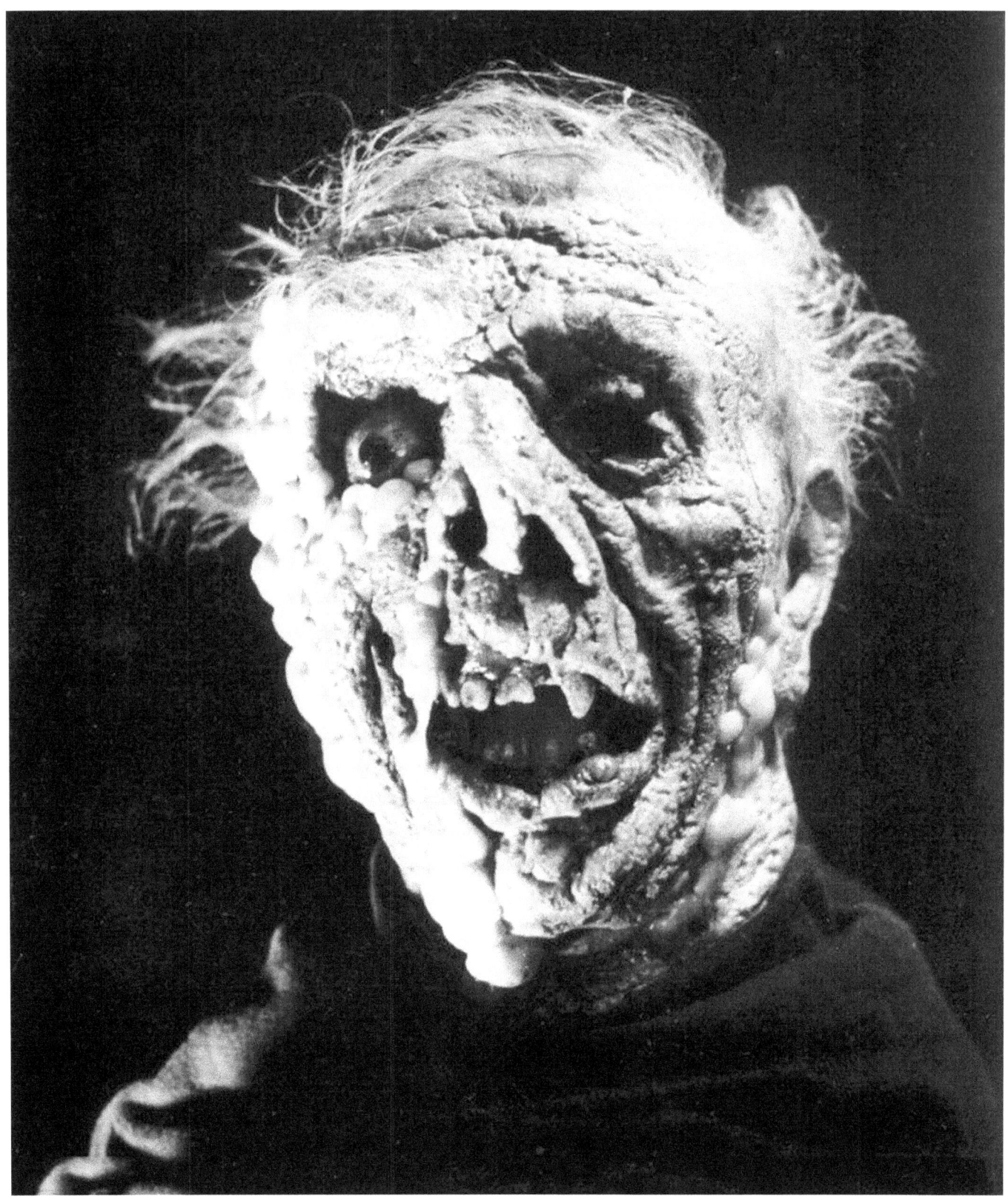

THE PICTURE OF DORIAN GRAY
Production: USA, 1961
Director: Paul Bogart
Category: Horror
Series 1, Episode 1 of the TV series **Golden Showcase**, whch ran fron 1961 to 1964.
Dick Smith created the hoffic make-up effects for the disintegrating Dorian.

PIT AND THE PENDULUM
Production: USA, 1961
Director: Roger Corman
Category: Horror
Corman's second Poe adaptation and the best, with Barbara Steele starring alongside Vincent Price and several great shock moments. A classic.

SHADOW OF THE CAT
Production: UK, 1961
Director: John Gilling
Category: Horror
Often listed as a Hammer film, although its production credits read BHP, **The Shadow Of The Cat** was directed by John Gilling, photographed in monochrome by Arthur Grant and made at Bray Studios, with Barbara Shelley in a leading role. A meditation upon Edgar Allan Poe's short story "The Black Cat", this unusual piece is somewhat overdrawn but noteworthy for its sustained expressionistic mood, using shadowplay to heighten its implications of horror.

URSULA
Production: USA, 1961
Director: Lloyd Michael Williams
Category: Horror/Experimental
Perhaps the best-known short (11 minutes) film by Williams, a queer experimental film-maker who produced a series of increasingly wild works throughout the 1960s, culminating in the controversial **Rainbow's Children**. **Ursula** is the tale of a young girl driven insane by an abusive mother, a fracturing conveyed by extreme camera angles, colour saturation, special effects and psychotronic music. From the horror story "Miss Gentilbelle" by Charles Beaumont.

YOURS TRULY, JACK THE RIPPER
Production: USA, 1961
Director: Ray Milland
Category: Horror/Science Fiction
Perhaps the most outstanding episode from the Boris Karloff-hosted US TV horror series **Thriller** (1960-62), based on the famous story by Robert Bloch (first published in *Weird Tales* in 1943) in which the world's most notorious serial killer may be staying young and alive by continuing his of spree of butchery for decade after decade. Bloch also scripted several other stand-out episides, including **The Cheaters**, directed by John Brahm, and **The Grim Reaper**, featuring William Shatner.

EL BARÓN DEL TERROR
("The Baron Of Terror")
Production: Mexico, 1962
Director: Chano Urueta
US release title: **The Brainiac**
Category: Horror

CARNIVAL OF SOULS
Production: USA, 1962
Director: Herk Hervey
Category: Horror/Trance

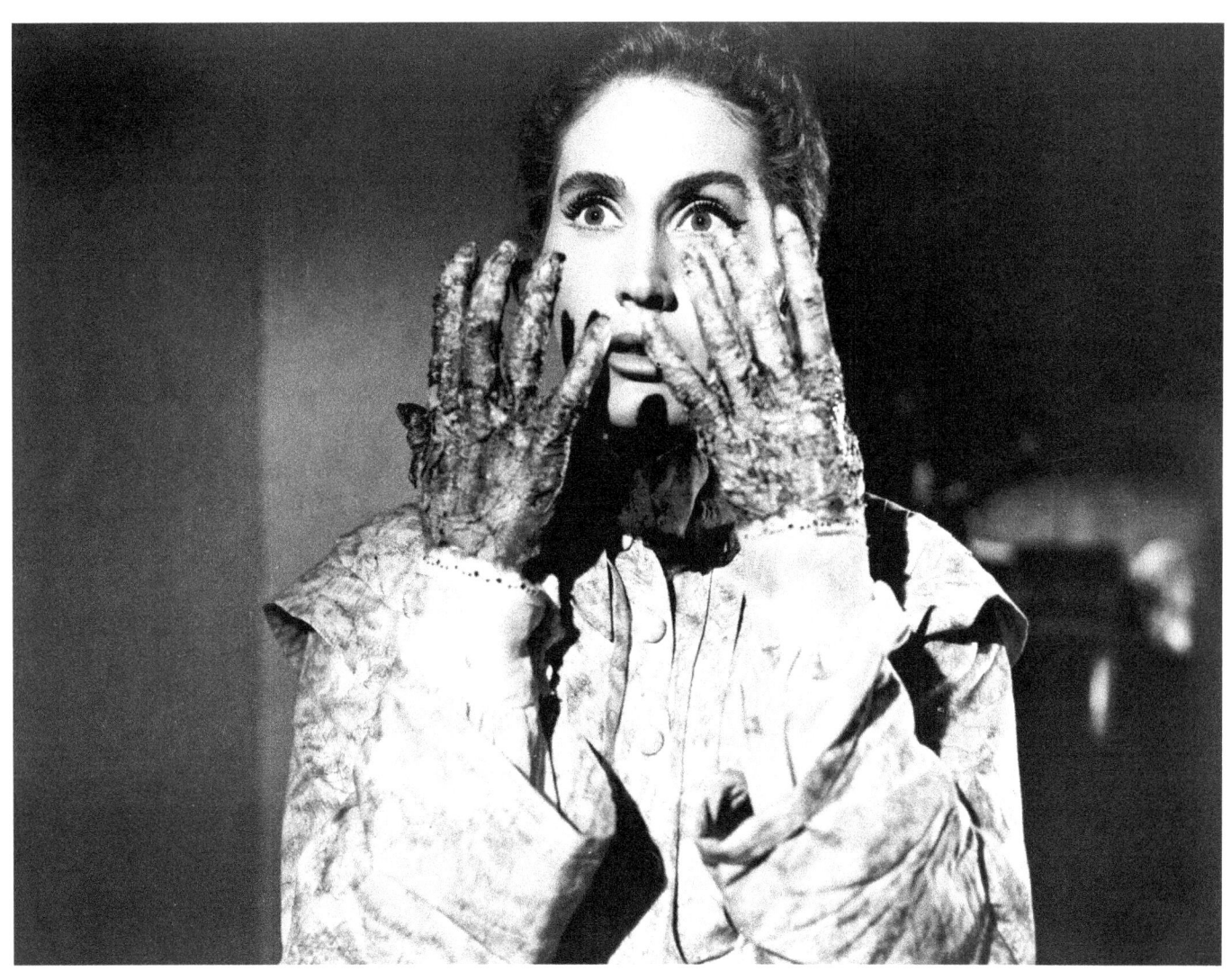

EL ESPEJO DE LA BRUJA
("The Witch's Mirror")
Production: Mexico, 1962
Director: Chano Urueta
Category: Horror
Urueta's most effective horror movie, the tale of a witch who uses a demonic mirror to conjure up hellish retribution upon her murderous employer. Magic rituals, grave desecration and disfigurement feature among the film's range of dark oneiric imagery as the man's dead wife is resurrected in the form of a vengeful ghost. Some sources cite a 1960 production date for this film.

FANTASMAGORIE
(Patrice Molinard, 1962: France)
("Phantasmagoria")
Production: /France, 1962
Director: Patrice Molinard
Category: Horror/Fantasy
A 40-minute vampire film featuring Edith Scob, spectral star of the classic **Les Yeux Sans Visage**.

GRITOS EN LA NOCHE
("Screams In The Night")
Production: Spain/France, 1962
Director: Jésus Franco
US release title: **The Awful Dr. Orlof**
Category: Horror
Franco's first film portrayal of the Sadean surgeon Orlof, a medical figure whose activities are conflated with the sexual and perverse. In a tale ripped off from Franju's **Les Yeux Sans Visage**, Orlof (played by Howard Vernon) abducts prostitutes and strippers so he may use their skin to repair his daughter's disfigured face, aided by his mutant servant Morpho. Weird camera angles, eerie music and stark black-and-white photography make this a minor nouveau-gothic classic. Franco went on to specialize in horror films, with more and more sex and perversion added; 1964's sequel, **El Secreto Del Dr. Orloff**, for example, contains as much nudity and voyeurism as the censors would allow. Orlof became a recurring figure in Spanish trash horror cinema; Howard Vernon reprised the role in Santos Alcocer's **El Enigma Del Ataúd** (1967), Pierre Chevalier's sleazy **La Vie Amoureuse De L'Homme Invisible** (1970), and Franco's **El Siniestro Doctor Orloff** (1984) and **Faceless** (1989), a blood-drenched remake of **Gritos En La Noche**. Orlof was also played by William Berger in Franco's **Los Ojos Siniestros Del Doctor Orloff** (1973).

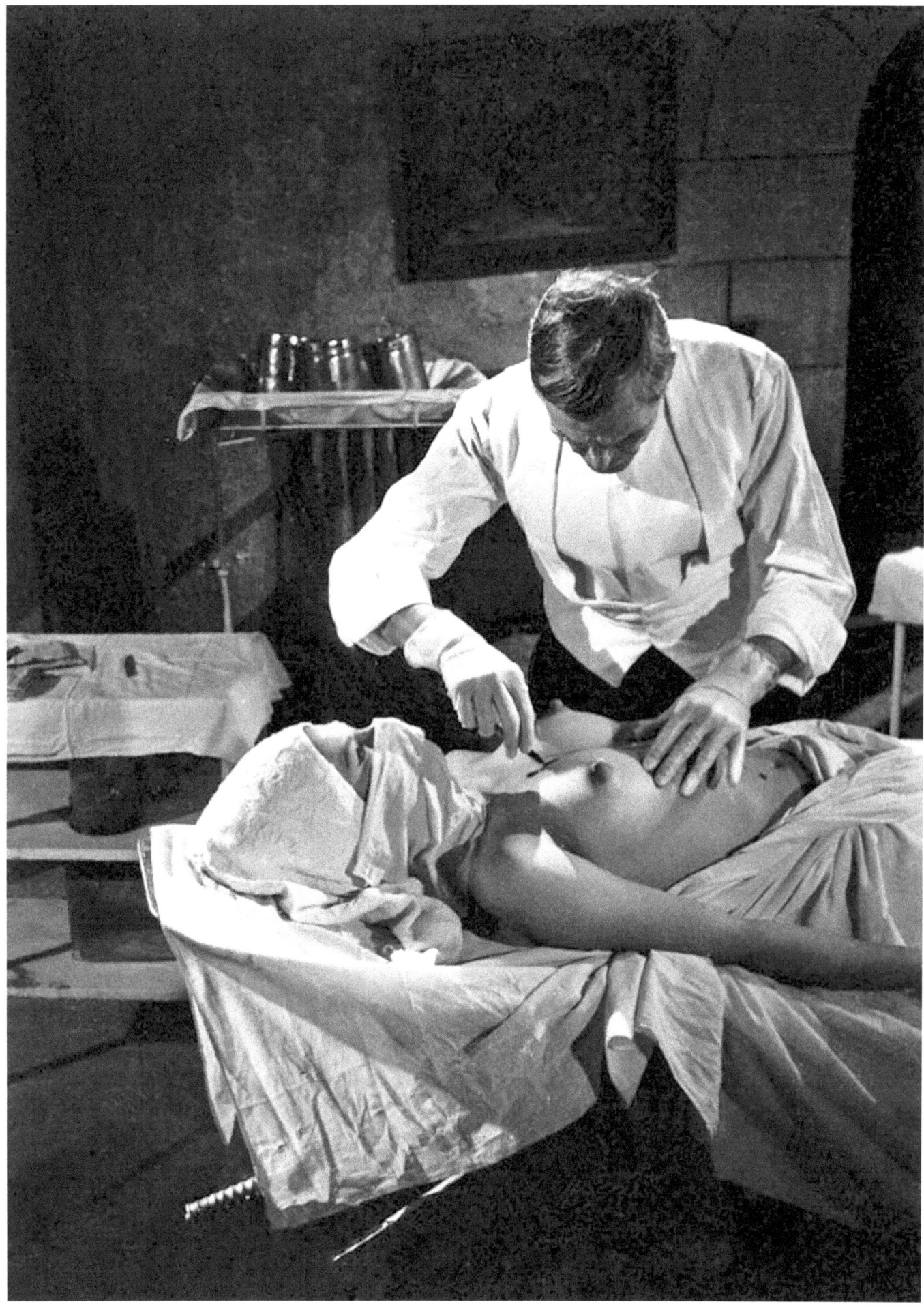

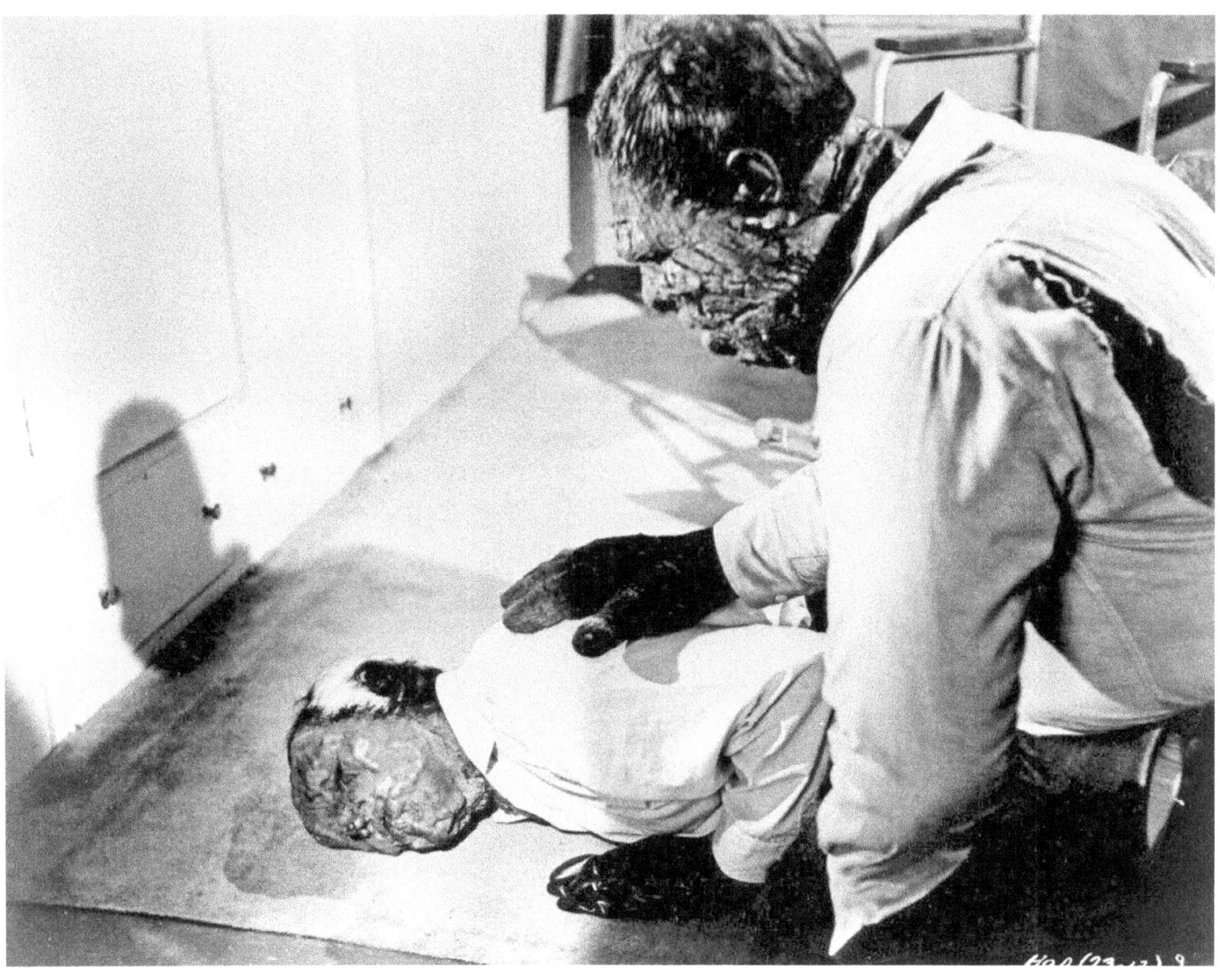

HAND OF DEATH
Production: USA, 1962
Director: Gene Nelson
Category: Horror/Science Fiction

HUANG MAO GUIREN
("Yellow Hair Monster")
Production: Hong Kong, 1962
Director: Wong Fung
Category: Horror

Pulp Cantonese cinema from the early 60s, the last and most outlandish in a series of films, which started in 1959, to feature the character of Wong Ang the Flying Heroine Bandit, who first appeared in the 1940s pulp novels of Siu Ping. As in all of the films, Wong Ang is played by martial arts queen Yu So-chow, but here is joined by rising starlets Connie Chan (just fifteen at the time) and Chan Ho-kau as her feisty sidekicks. The plot of **Huang Mao Guiren** involves a crazed scientist who creates the monster of the title using oran-utang blood, and plans to make it invincible by next weaning it onto human haemoglobin. The film also has corpses dissolved in acid, a ghost and a vampire, rape, murder, betrayal and revenge. Connie Chan went on to star in scores of films, perhaps most notably in the "Jane Bond" genre of girl-angled pulp costume spy thrillers such as Chor Yuen's **The Black Rose** (1965), Cheung Wai-Gwong's **Lady Black Cat** (1966), and Kangshi Mu's **Lady Bond** (1966); Jane Bond cinema was a mid-60s HK phenomenon of which the Wong Ang films can be seen as a significant precursor.

NIGHT OF THE EAGLE
Production: UK, 1962
Director: Sidney Hayers
US release title: **Burn Witch Burn**
Category: Horror/Witchcraft

L'ORRIBILE SEGRETO DEL DR. HICHCOCK
("Dr. Hitchcock's Horrible Secret")
Production: Italy, 1962
Director: Riccardo Freda
Category: Horror
Colour-saturated paean to necrophilia which rivals Bava in its gothic glory. Featuring Barbara Steele, the neurasthenic sex queen of Italian horror, this morbid and lurid fusion of Poe and Krafft-Ebing remains a true cult classic. "The candle of his lust burnt brightest in the shadow of the grave!" Also known as **Raptus**.

THE PHANTOM OF THE OPERA
Production: UK, 1962
Director: Terence Fisher
Category: Horror

Hammer's remake is fairly uninspired, with the most notable twist being the inclusion of a homicidal dwarf (Ian Wilson, also seen in **The Wicker Man**). Herbert Lom took the title role that Lon Chaney and Claude Rains had assumed in earlier versions, while Heather Sears played the young opera singer to whom the Phantom gives her big chance, and whose life he saves by sacrificing his own. Compared to Chaney, Lom's make-up is rather disappointing (his face is disfigured by acid), and only the eerie splendour of the Phantom's underground lair is fully realised. All in all, a rather pointless reworking – as were all the numerous versions that followed (including the bizarre **Phantom Of The Paradise**, a Faustian rock musical starring singing dwarf Paul Williams).

THE PIT
Production: UK, 1962
Director: Edward Abrahams
Category: Horror
A pure cinematic adaptation of Poe's "Pit And The Pendulum", lasting 30 minutes and with only one word of dialogue. The claustrophobic horror of a man chained motionless to a table as the razor-edged blade swings ever closer to his belly is conveyed purely by sound effects and visual horror, the bottom of the pit piled high with the rotting bones of the damned. A film financed by the Experimental Film Fund and rated "X" by the British censor.

THE PREMATURE BURIAL
Production: USA, 1962
Director: Roger Corman
Category: Horror
The third and one of the least-seen in Corman's Poe cycle (mainly because Vincent Price is absent), **The Premature Burial** stars Ray Milland as the cataleptic suffering from a stifling fear of being buried alive. With beautifully morbid sets and colour schemes, plus the customary Corman dream-sequence, this is one of the better, least hysterical films in Corman's series.

LA RIVIÈRE DU HIBOU
("Owl River")
Production: France, 1962
Director: Robert Enrico
Category: Horror

A 30-minute adaptation of Ambrose Bierce's famous short story "An Occurrence at Owl Creek Bridge", which has inspired many films – from **The Bridge** to **Jacob's Ladder** and beyond – but seldom under its original title. Enrico's version is beautifully crafted, and the shock ending still retains its power. Originally part of a three-part portmanteau movie of Bierce stories, **Au Coeur De La Vie, La Rivière Du Hibou** was promoted as a stand-alone film and won the 1962 Oscar for Best Short Subject. It was subsequently screened as an episode of **The Twilight Zone** TV series.

SANTO CONTRA LAS MUJERES VAMPIRO
("Santo Versus The Vampire Women")
Production: Mexico, 1962
Director: Alfonso Corona Blake
Category: Horror

Pehaps the best, and certainly the best known, of the horror films starring *luchador* El Santo. The set design and sequences featuring resurrected, facially disfigured vampires and the vampire queen, Zorina, herself, are effective, and even Satan appears, represented in silhouette. Sadly, the mood is inevitably ruined by other scenes featuring the masked wrestler, both in and out of the ring, which was indeed the case with all of the Santo films. Like many Mexican fantasy films of this period, **Santo Contra Las Mujeres Vampiro** was imported for US distribution by entrepreneur K. Gordon Murray, who dubbed, edited, retitled and released it as **Samson Vs. The Vampire Women** in 1963 – a version to be avoided. Meanwhile, Santo continued with a deluge of horror-related films; amongst his next adventures were **Santo En El Museo de Cera** (1963), **Santo En Atacan Las Brujas** (1964), **Santo En Los Profanadores De Tumbas** (1965), and **Santo Contra La Invasión De Los Marcianos** (1966), the latter often viewed as the trash pinnacle of his 60s output.

LA STRAGE DEI VAMPIRI
("The Vampire Massacre")
Production: Italy, 1962
Director: Roberto Mauri
US release title: **Curse Of The Blood Ghouls**
Category: Horror

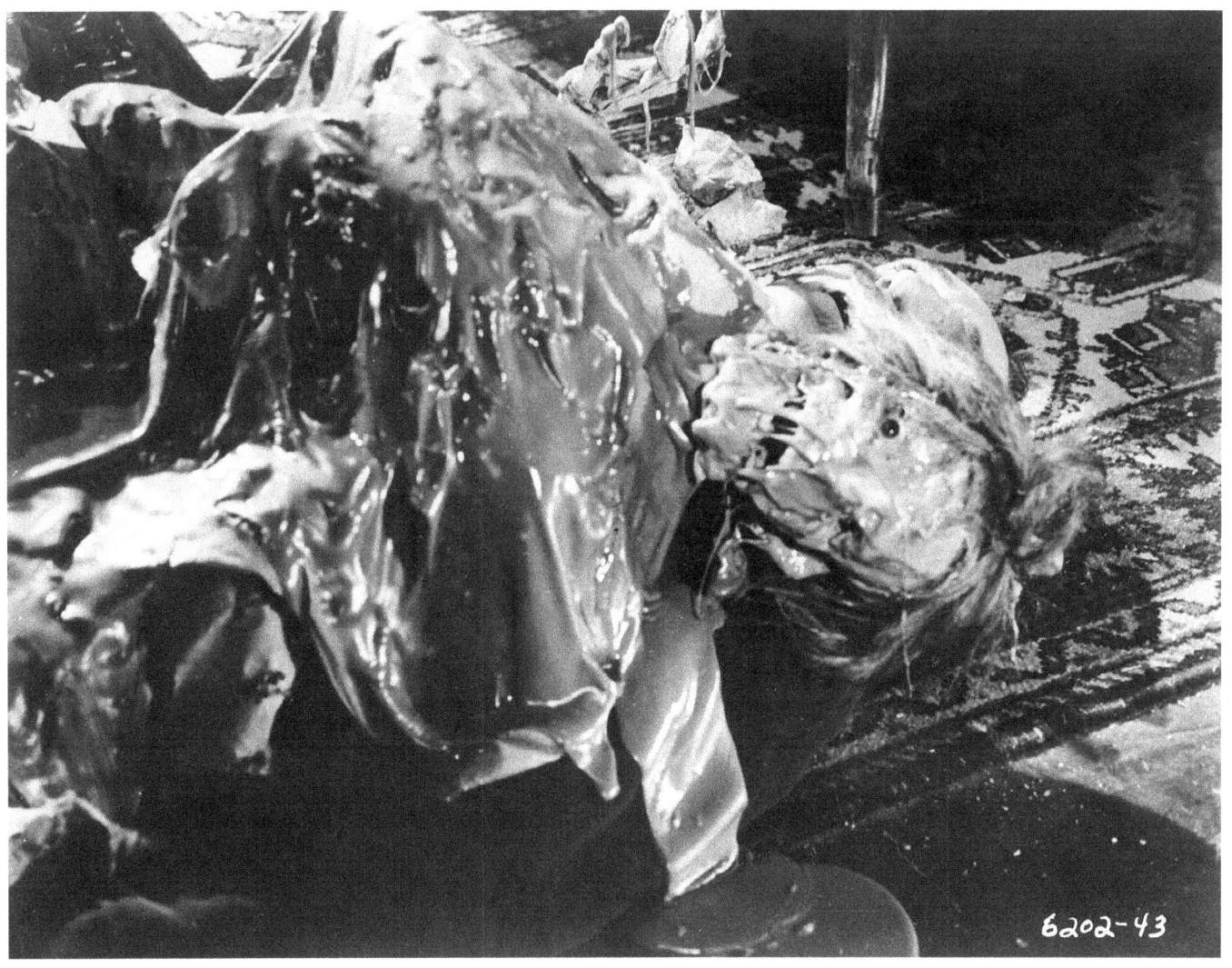

TALES OF TERROR
Production: USA, 1962
Director: Roger Corman
Category: Horror
The fourth entry in Corman's classic Poe film cycle, collecting author's tales "Morella", "The Facts In The Case Of M. Valdemar", and a mingling of "The Black Cat" with "The Cask Of Amontillado". Vincent Price stars in all three segments, which – sadly – are more light-hearted in tone than the director's earlier three Poe movies.

EL VAMPIRO SANGRIENTE
("The Blood-Soaked Vampire")
Production: Mexico, 1962
Director: Miguel Morayta
Category: Horror
The first of two vampire films by Morayta, in which the vampire-hunter Count Cagliostro pursues the destruction of Count Frankenhausen, a blood-drinker engaged in the slaughter and exsanguination of young virgins. This was followed in 1963 by a sequel, **La Invasion De Los Vampiros**.

KYONETSU NO KISETSU
("Season Of Wild Lusts")
Production: Japan, 1960
Director: Koreyoshi Kurahara
English release title: **The Warped Ones**
Category: Juvenile Delinquency

MAYHEM

À BOUT DE SOUFFLE
("Out Of Breath")
Production: France, 1960
Director: Jean-Luc Godard
English release title: **Breathless**
Category: Crime/Nihilism

This was Godard's breakthrough film. Jean-Paul Belmondo and Jean Seberg play a young couple being pursued by police; the film is precipitous, propelled by jump-cuts, and shows complete contempt for both society and cinematic convention. The first masterpiece of the French New Wave, an annihilatory arc of violent life on collision course with death.

DIE BANDE DES SCHRECKENS
("The Terror Gang")
Production: Germany, 1960
Director: Harald Reinl
Category: Krimi

Reinl's second film in the Rialto/Edgar Wallace pulp crime series, based on the novel *The Terrible People*, is a beautifully photographed, corpse-strewn gothic *gruselkrimi* in which an executed criminal apparently returns from the dead and exacts murderous vengeance on his persecutors. Reinl's next film in the series would be **Der Falscher Von London** (1961), followed by **Zimmer 13** in 1963; during this period he also directed two notable pseudo-Wallace entries for other companies: **Der Teppich des Grauens** and **Der Weisse Spinne**.

DEN BLODIGA TIDEN
("The Age Of Blood")
Production: Sweden, 1960
Director: Erwin Leiser
English release title: **Mein Kampf**
Category: Atrocity

Another searing testament to the meteoric rise of Hitler, including graphic, previously unseen concentration camp footage from the private vaults of Goebbels – apparently a keen amateur film-maker. **Den Blodiga Tiden** was produced by Tore Sjoberg, who directed the Swedish production **Krigsförbrytare** ("War Criminal") in 1956; this harrowing documentary, which includes footage of mass extermination and dismembered bodies from the Nazi Death Camps, was notable as the first film to expose the horrors of Ilse Koch and her collection of human skin ornaments, revealing her to be no "mere" war criminal, but a genuine female psychopath torturing, killing and skinning her victims under cover of night and fog. Also with archive film of Ilse Koch, Josef Goebbels, Adolf Hitler, Heinrich Himmler, Irma Grese, and many others. In 1963 Sjoberg directed/produced **The Face Of War**, which included footage from Hiroshima and Nagasaki.

IL GOBBO
("The Hunchback")
Production: Italy/France, 1960
Director: Carlo Lizzani
Category: Crime
An early acting role for Pier Paolo Pasolini in this neo-realist blast of "machine-gun" cinema, in which a hunchbacked freedom fighter in Nazi-occupied Rome (played by Gérard Blain) helps drive out the invaders with his bullet-spraying teenage cohorts, only to gather together a gang of 150 criminals and rule over a poor suburb of the liberated city. He is finally killed by police in a hail of gunfire.

HELL IS A CITY
Production: UK, 1960
Director: Val Guest
Category: Crime
Notable Hammer Films production, a unusually tough urban *noir* thriller shot in Manchester and starring Stanley Baker as the police inspector tracking down a jailbreaker who turns murderer and coping with a frigid nagging wife who resents the time he spends on his work. Actress Billie Whitelaw was involved in a moment of discreet nudity that was quite surprising for a British film of that period.

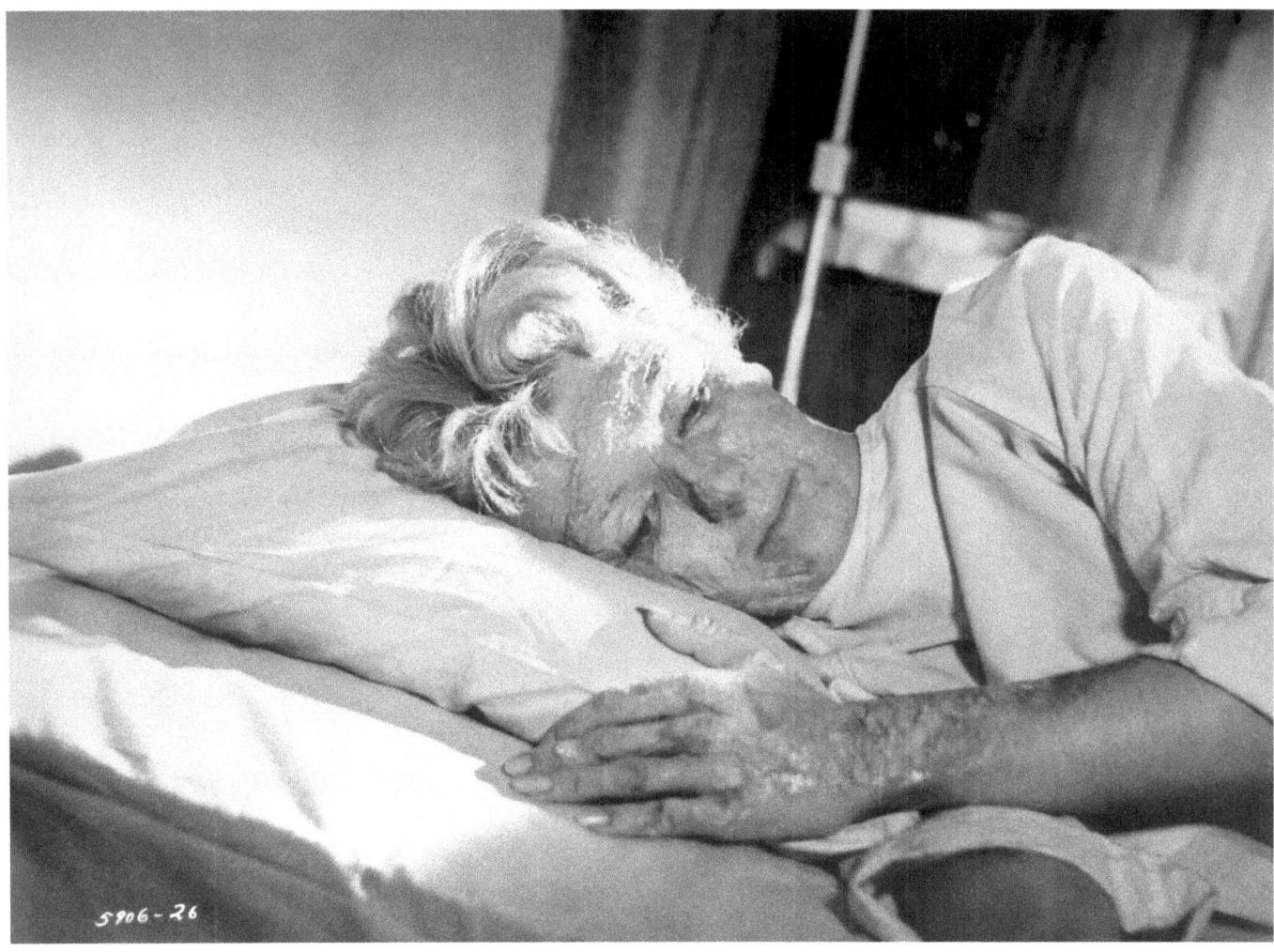

THE HYPNOTIC EYE
Production: USA, 1960
Director: George Blair
Category: Mayhem/Horror
Desmond, a maniacal hypnotist, uses his powers to make a series of women mutilate and disfigure their own faces, incluidng self-blinding and bathing in acid.

KAPO
Production: France/Italy, 1960
Director: Gillo Pontecorvo
Category: Nazism/Atrocity
An early entry in a genre that had not yet been fully recognized, though later identified as an "exploitation piece", **Kapò** is set in a Nazi concentration camp and investigates cruelty to female prisoners. A teenaged Jewish girl, played by Susan Strasberg, is arrested by the SS and sent to a brutal camp, where she becomes a "kapo", one of the auxiliary guards recruited from the inmates, and is corrupted by the power she now has over her fellow captives. However, when a friend dies she repents and perishes leading an escape attempt. With scenes of women being hanged, **Kapò** is an early, mild glimpse at fictionalised death kamp atrocity cinema.

KEY WITNESS
Production: USA, 1960
Director: Phil Karlson
Category: Crime

MA BARKER'S KILLER BROOD
Production: USA, 1960
Director: Bill Karn
Category: Crime

A blazing pulp inferno of pumping machine-guns and incendiary violence, not only tracking the bloody life and crimes of Ma Barker and her sons, but throwing in fellow outlaws John Dillinger, Baby Face Nelson and Machine-Gun Kelly to make up a fearsome juggernaut of vice. The film was refused certification by the British censor at time of release – a good indication of its subversive power. Karn also directed **Five Minutes To Live** (1961), which featured Johnny Cash in a rare (and maniacal) acting

role as a psychopathic bank robber. Barker was also the inspiration for "Ma Webster" in **Queen Of The Mob** (1940), and "Ma Jarrett", one half of the Oedipal mother-son relationship in the terminal gangster-noir movie **White Heat** (1949).

THE POLICE AND THE MENTALLY ILL
Production: USA, 1960
Category: Documentary/Crime
An educational film from the US Police Department, showing police officers how to deal with mentally deranged criminals or suspects, such as the woman who thinks her heart's been cut out, violent teenagers hopped up on bop pills, or mad bombers. A similar film is **Booked For Safekeeping** (1960), co-produced by the Louisiana Association for Mental Health.

PSYCHO
Production: USA, 1960
Director: Alfred Hitchcock
Category: Maniac

Hitchcock formally invents the slasher movie, incorporating motifs which are now cliché: the mother-fixated killer/transvestite knife maniac, women stalked and slaughtered as punishment for their sexuality, the gothic house on the hill, nerve-shredding score, and other tropes. With some good sick moments. Joseph Stefano adapted the novel by Robert Bloch, which was in turn inspired by the case of Ed Gein, the Wisconsin cannibal-necrophile. Whereas Gein had adorned himself in a suit and mask of his dead mother's skin to dance by moonlight, Hitchcock's insane protagonist Norman Bates (Anthony Perkins) was content to stuff his mother's body and keep it preserved in a top bedroom. The real trouble starts when Bates, blasted by Oedipal guilt, imagines she is still alive and issuing directives to slay young women to whom he is sexually attracted. Finally her personality engulfs him, and we see Bates possessed, her skull superimposed over his face, a living testament to familial sickness. Although at first met with a degree of critical ridicule, **Psycho** rightly later assumed the status of absolute classic, so much so that over twenty years later, three inferior sequels appeared: **Psycho II** (1983), **Psycho III** (1986, directed by Perkins, star of the original film), and **Psycho IV: The Beginning** (1990). Even more bizarrely, Gus van Sant made a totally pointless scene-for-scene colour remake in 1996.

DER RACHER
("The Avenger")
Production: Germany, 1960
Director: Karl Anton
Category: Krimi

Merging plotlines from two separate Edgar Wallace novels, *The Hairy Arm* and *The Avenger*, this *gruselkrimi* challenges the viewer to decide which (if either) of two sinister figures – a vigilante dispensing violent summary justice to criminals, or a crazed ape-creature on the loose – is stalking London's social elite and decapitating them one by one. **Der Racher** marked the first appearance in this Rialto-produced series by a young actor named Klaus Kinski; he would go on to appear in around seventeen more episodes, usually cast in shady roles, providing the springboard for his notorious international career in genre cinema and debauchery.

THE RISE AND FALL OF LEGS DIAMOND
Production: USA, 1960
Director: Budd Boetticher
Category: Crime

SEISHUN ZANKOKU MONOGATARI
("Cruel Story Of Youth")
Production: Japan, 1960
Director: Nagisa Oshima
Category: Juvenile Delinquency

The second film by Oshima, following his debut **Ai To Kibo No Machi** (1959), is a crystallization of the themes he had previously begun to develop. Inspired both by *taiyozoku* ("sun tribe") films such as **Kurutta Kajitsu** and by Marxist theory, Oshima's focus was on youth crime, gangs and abusive relationships, using them to comment on the state of contemporary Japan. His next film was the pessimistic **Taiyo No Hakaba** (1960), and these three debut films established him as a leader of the emergent New Wave of Japanese cinema, alongside others such as Masahiro Shinoda, Yoshishige Yoshida and Imamura Shohei. It was a common theme in the films of these three directors – the rebel or criminal gang – which would enable the birth of the 60s *yazuka* ("gangster") film genre – a genre which Shinoda himself, in particular,

would exploit and subvert with films like **Kawaita Hana** (1964). Oshima's more overtly political **Nihon No Yoru To Kiri** (1960) was quickly withdrawn by Shochiku due to its controversial nature, prompting him to quit the studio and direct **Shiiku** (1961) and **Amakusa Shiro Tokisada** (1962) independently.

THE SUBTERRANEANS
Production: USA, 1960
Director: Ranald McDougall
Category: Beat Movement
The first of Jack Kerouac's beatnik novels to be filmed, in an exploitation treatment which focuses on the trope of "wild youth".

DIE 1000 AUGEN DES DR, MABUSE
("The 1000 Eyes Of Dr. Mabuse")
Production: Germany/Italy/France, 1960
Director: Fritz Lang
Category: Krimi

In his last ever film, produced by German company CCC, Lang returned to a seminal character from his days as a film-maker in Berlin: Dr. Mabuse, the criminal mastermind. Anticipating many of the tropes which would mark out the future James Bond series, Lang presents a clandestine world of guns, girls, crime, fast cars, hidden cameras, subterranean lairs, agents of the law and crazed, megalomaniac villains. The film's title refers to the vast bank of television monitor screens through which Mabuse controls his evil empire, but might also be an ironic comment on the director's then-state of encroaching blindness. The success of **Die 1000 Augen Des Dr. Mabuse** spurred CCC into producing a number of sequels; these were: Harald Reinl's **Im Stahlnetz Des Dr. Mabuse** (1961) and **Die Unsichtbaren Krallen Des Dr. Mabuse** (1961), Werner Klinger's remake of **Das Testament Des Dr. Mabuse** (1962), Paul May's **Scotland Yard Jagt Dr. Mabuse** (1963 – from an original screenplay by Bryan Edgar Wallace), and Hugo Fregonese's **Des Todesstrahlen Des Dr. Mabuse** (1964). Maverick exploitation director Jesus Franco delivered a late coda, the Spanish/German co-production **La Venganza Del Dr. Mabuse**), in 1971.

TOO HOT TO HANDLE
Production: UK, 1960
Director: Terence Young
US release title: **Playgirl After Dark**
Category: Crime
Jayne Mansfield stars as a stripper caught up in the "crime-infested" Soho nightclub scene. With Christopher Lee.

AFTER MEIN KAMPF
Production: USA, 1961
Director: Ralph Porter
Alternative title: **Ravaged**
Category: Atrocity
Semi-documentary on Hitler's rise to power and the atrocities committed by his Nazi henchmen. Includes footage of Majdenek extermination camp, plus restagings of rape and murder by SS guards, and experiments in which prostitutes were used to revive near-frozen prisoners. "Hitler's sadists leave their shameless mark! Ravages you never dreamed possible this side of Hell!"

BLAST OF SILENCE
Production: USA, 1961
Director: Allen Baron
Category: Crime Noir
A late film noir which has become a cult classic, **Blast Of Silence** revolves around Frankie, a hate-filled hit-man who is hired to kill a mob boss but then gets double-crossed by his employers. This simple plot is vastly enhanced by the style of the movie, which features schizophrenic voice-overs that seem to be boiling inside Frankie's head, compounding his existential desolation, as he moves through the bleak New York locations, finally meeting his fate on a hurricane-swept Long Island waterfront.

BLOODLUST!
Production: USA, 1961
Director: Ralph Brooke
Category: Murder/Maniac
Yet another variation on the theme of **The Most Dangerous Game**.

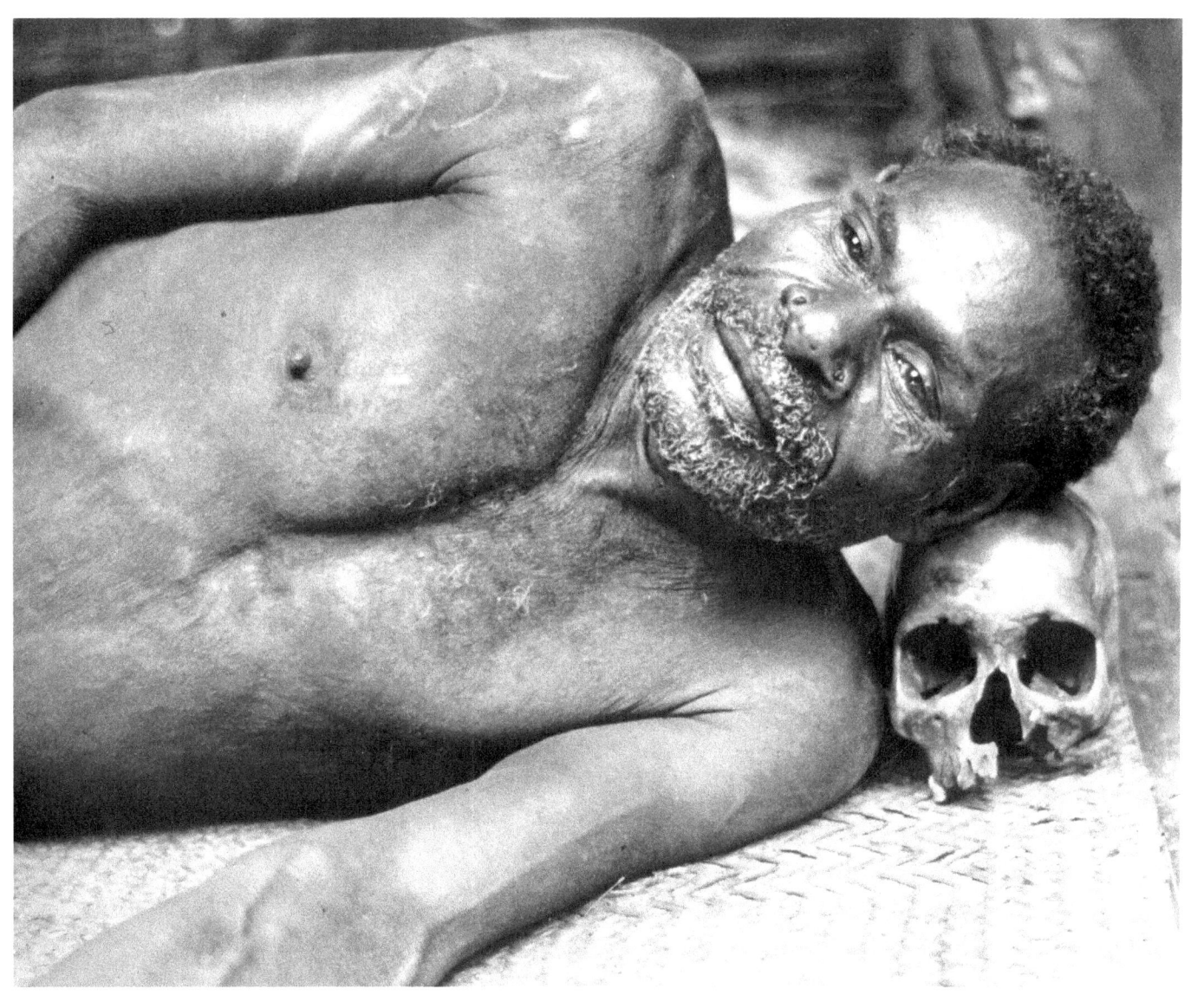

LE CIEL ET LA BOUE
("Sky And Mud")
Production: France, 1961
Director: Pierre-Dominique Gaisseau
Category: Ethno-Documentary

THE CONNECTION
Production: USA, 1961
Director: Shirley Clarke
Category: Drug Addiction

Controversial film by Clarke that focused on drug addiction, as opposed to dance or cityscapes which were the main concern of her earlier, shorter studies such as **Dance In The Sun** or **Bridges-Go-Round**. Based on a theatre play, **The Connection** depicts one day in the life of a group of junkies in a downtown loft; they are shown in idle discussion, playing jazz, nodding out, eating and drinking, and other various ways in which addicts spend their basically formless time, a lack of structure reflected in the film itself. Clarke's constantly mobile camera contributed a strong element of stylistic innovation, but the film's foul language, subject matter and non-narrative format contributed to much negative reaction, including a one-year ban by the New York State censorship board. It is now regarded as a key work of the New American Cinema of the 1960s.

FURYO SHONEN
("Juvenile Delinquents")
Production: Japan, 1961
Director: Susumu Hani
Category: Juvenile Delinquency

The first feature by director Hani was set in a reform school for boys, and he invested the film with a semi-documentary realism by using delinquent youths who had actually served time, and letting them improvise in front of the camera. The result was an intriguing counterpoint to the exploitational "sun tribe" dramas being produced by Nikkatsu and other studios, and indicated another way not only to tackle the subject of alienated youth, but also to create an engaging new cinema. Hani went on to co-direct, with Giuliano Tomei, one of the first "mondo" movies set in Japan – **Il Paradiso Dell'Uomo: Giappone Proibito** (1963). Another Japanese mondo from the same year was **Nihon Zankoku Monogatari**, directed by Nobuo Nakagawa, Haku Komori, and Ten Takahashi.

DAS GEHEIMNIS DER GELBEN NARZISSEN
("The Mystery Of The Yellow Daffodils")
Production: Germany/UK, 1961
Director: Ákos Ráthonyi
Category: Krimi

From the Edgar Wallace novel of the same name, this *gruselkrimi* features not only Klaus Kinski, but also horror star Christopher Lee in a tale of security forces versus narcotics and sex traffickers, plus a shadowy serial killer at work in the city's seedy underbelly. This was Rialto's first UK co-production, and German and English language versions were shot simultaneously. **Das Geheimnis Der Gelben Narzissen** lacks the gothic/macabre tone of most other films in the series but, with its stocking-masked killer, torture, vicious stabbings and other acts of brutal violence, often anticipates aspects of the Italian *giallo*. Lee and Kinski would both be back for **Das Rätsel Der Roten Orchidee** that same year, whilst Rialto would engage in just two further UK collaborations: **Traitor's Gate** (1964, directed by Freddie Francis), and **The Trygon Factor** (Cyril Frankel, 1966), concerning a sect of sinister nuns.

HOMICIDAL
Production: USA, 1961
Director: William Castle
Category: Maniac

THE JIVARO SHRINK A HUMAN HEAD
Production: Ecuador/Poland, 1961
Director: Edmundo Bielawski
Category: Ethno-Documentary
A rare filmic capture of the gruesome head-shrinking culture once prevalent in South America.

MECHANIZED DEATH
Production: USA, 1961
Director: Richard Wayman
Category: Documentary/Auto-Mayhem
Real-life footage of autovehicular carnage supplied by the Ohio Highway Patrol, featuring the pulped, mangled, dismembered and immolated corpses of reckless drivers and their victims.

PORTRAIT OF A MOBSTER
Production: USA, 1961
Director: Joseph Pevney
Category: Crime
Biopic of gangster Dutch Schultz, who is perhaps now best-known for his fevered dying words, around which William S. Burroughs fashioned a text in 1969. When asked by police how many shots were fired at him, Schultz replied: "Two thousand. Come one, get some money in that treasury. We need it. Come on, please get it. I can't tell you to. That is not what you have in the book. Oh, please warden. What am I going to do for money? Please put me up on my feet at once. You are a hard boiled man. Did you hear me? I would hear it, the Circuit Court would hear it, and

the Supreme Court might hear it. If that ain't the pay-off. Please crack down on the Chinaman's friends and Hitler's commander. I am sore and I am going up and I am going to give you honey if I can. Mother is the best bet and don't let Satan draw you too fast."

DIE SELTSAME GRAFIN
("The Strange Countess")
Production: Germany, 1961
Director: Josef Von Baky
Category: Krimi
Set in a gothic mansion owned by the bizarrely named Lord Moron, this Edgar Wallace *gruselkrimi* is a tale of torment, nightmares and incipient madness. With regular player Klaus Kinski, and based on the Wallace novel *The Sins Of The Mother*.

THE SINISTER URGE
Production: USA, 1961
Director: Ed Wood Jr
Category: Maniac
Among the first examples of Wood's transition from trash horror to sex-based exploitation themes. "A photograph by mail. A compulsive urge. A slash of a knife."

LA TARANTA
Production: Italy, 1961
Director: Gianfranco Mengozzi
Category: Documentary/Mondo
Documentary that captures Italian peasant women in trances and paroxysms of magico-religious ecstasy, the so-called "tarantella" performed to cure spider-bites. Mengozzi had previously recorded the equally primal bull-running rites at Pamplona, in **Festa A Pamplona** (1959). A later evocation of tarantism was Gabriella Rosaleva's **La Sposa Di San Paolo** (aka **Tarantula**, 1989), recreating the hysterical demonic possession and exorcisms which existed in Southern Italy in the 16th and 17th centuries, all supposedly deriving from bites.

TASTE OF FEAR
Production: UK, 1961
Director: Seth Holt
Category: Psycho-Thriller
In the aftermath of Hitchcock's **Psycho** and Henri Clouzot's **Les Diaboliques**, Hammer were among the many to embark upon a series of horror-tinged psychological thrillers. **Taste Of Fear** was an auspicious first entry into the field, taking a fairly cliché'd storyline (a conspiracy to drive a young girl insane) and endowing it with new life, wringing out every last drop of suspense, some not inconsiderable shocks and a series of unguessable plot twists. Penny Appleton (played by Susan Strasberg) is the heroine, a frightened young woman in a wheelchair visiting her father at his French villa. Her stepmother (Anne Todd) insists that he is away, but his dead body keeps appearing... Hammer continued in this sub-genre with shock films like **Paranoiac, Maniac,** and **Nightmare**.

THE TERROR OF THE TONGS
Production: UK, 1961
Director: Anthony Bushell
Category: Sadism/Secret Sects

Hammer's **Terror Of The Tongs** was a tale of Hong Kong's Red Dragon Tong of 1919 – a murderous secret sect engaged in white slavery and opium smuggling. The film's hero eventually avenges his daughter's death by bringing down the Tong leader Chung King (Christopher Lee), but not before he has been subjected to such refined tortures as bone-scraping. Lee was warming up for his later portrayal of oriental fiend Fu Manchu in a series of films produced by Harry Alan Towers, starting with **The Face Of Fu Manchu** in 1965.

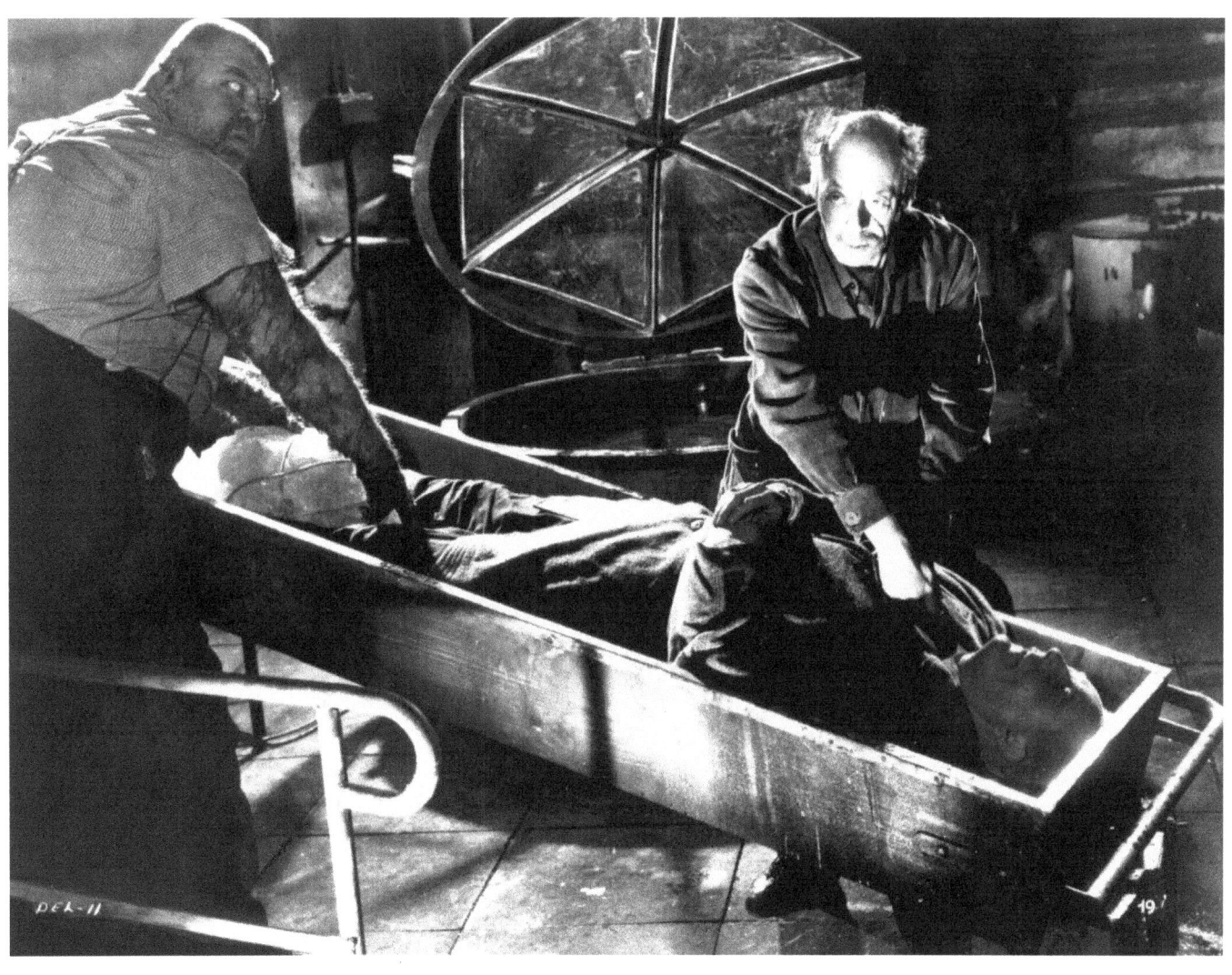

DIE TOTEN AUGEN VON LONDON
("Dead Eyes Of London")
Production: Germany, 1961
Director: Alfred Vohrer
Category: Krimi
The first Rialto/Edgar Wallace film to be directed by Vohrer, who would go on to virtually monopolise the series as the 60s progressed. Based on the novel *Dark Eyes Of London* (originally filmed in 1939 with Bela Lugosi), Vohrer's first *gruselkrimi* features Klaus Kinski in shades, alongside a huge, bald and blind strangler with a bestial hand. Elements from the same book would be used in Rialto's later **Der Gorilla Von Soho**.

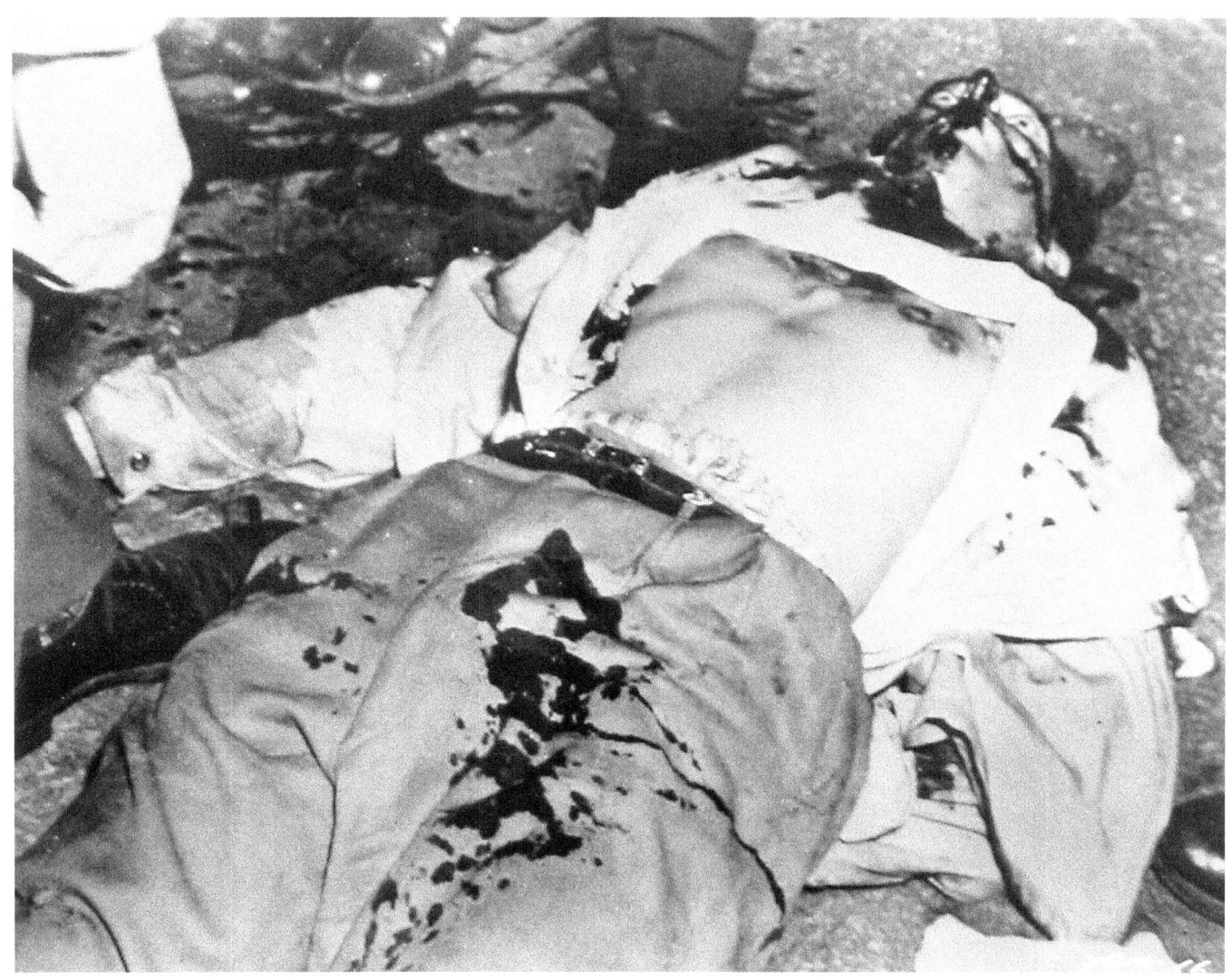

TRUE GANG MURDERS
Production: USA, 1961
Director: Sherman Rosenfield
Category: Crime/Murder

LES ABYSSES
("The Depths")
Production: France, 1962
Director: Nico Papatakis
Category: Murder

The strange case of the Papin Sisters remains one of the most sensational in French history. In 1933, these two maids suddenly and savagely turned on their employer, killing her and her daughter. It was an act of supreme carnage – eyes torn from sockets, faces pulped, genitals mutilated – and also an *"acte-gratuite"* of revolt that earned the Papins the eternal admiration of the Surrealist group. Papatakis' film of the case was described by Jean Genet as a "tornado from start to finish" and by Jean-Paul Sartre as the "first tragedy" of cinema, but it was attacked by the critics for bringing French cinema into disrepute. Genet's own play *Les Bonnes* ("The Maids") was strongly influenced by the Papin case and posits the two girls as enacting incestuous, sado-masochistic scenarios; it was filmed in 1974 by Christopher Miles as **The Maids**, with Glenda Jackson and Susannah York in the leading roles. Other, more radical interpretations of the Genet text include Robert and Donald Kinney's **The Maids**, which focuses on the characters' lesbian undertones (Genet original intention was for the two women to be played by men in drag), and Ildiko Szabo's **Maidsplay** (1983), an experimental piece by Nicole Dreiske's Facets Performance Ensemble which also incorporates transcripts from the original Papin murder trial.

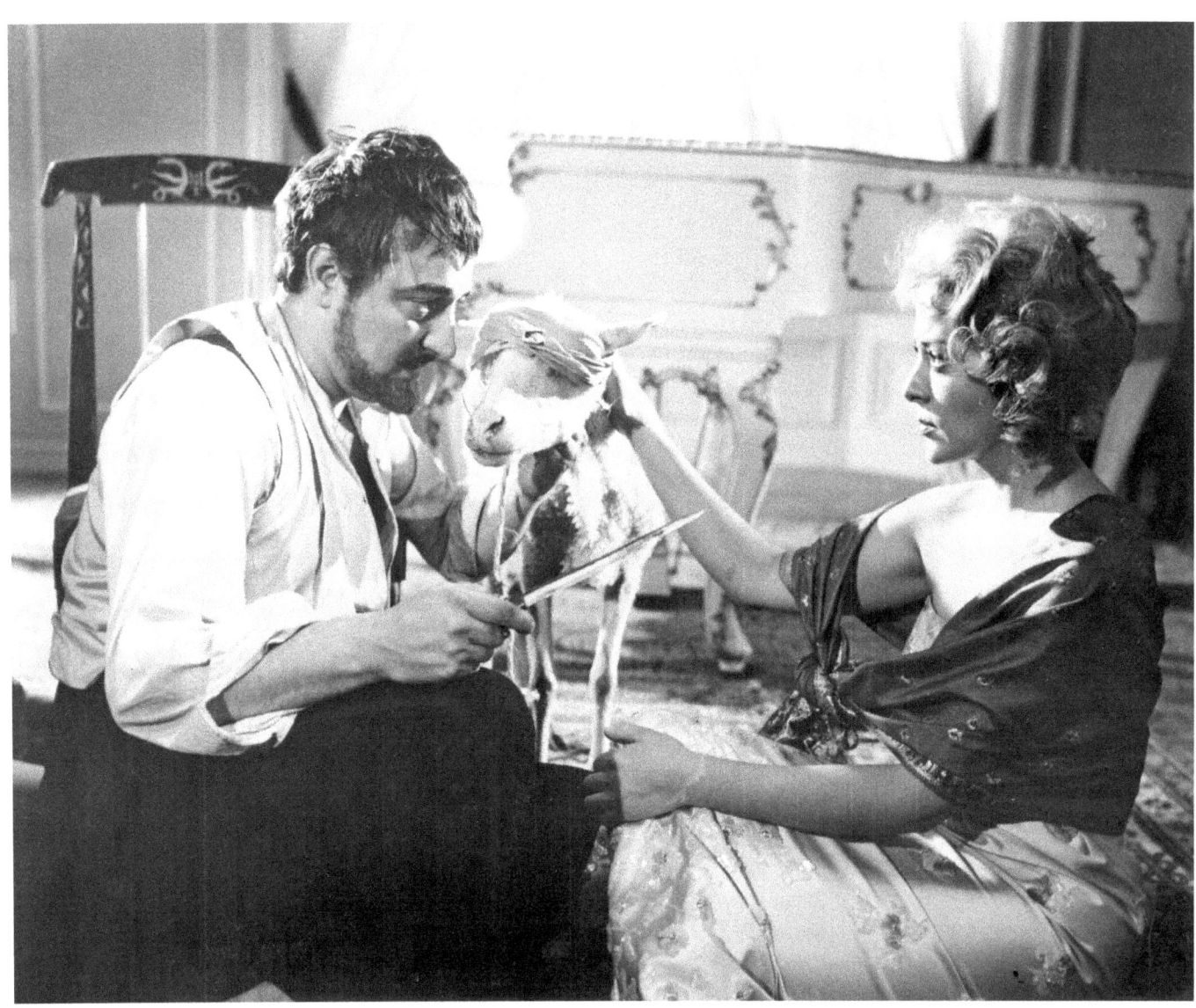

EL ÁNGEL EXTERMINADOR
("The Exterminating Angel")
Production: Mexico, 1962
Director: Luis Buñuel
Category: Absurdism
Buñuel's black comedy concerns a group of supposed sophisticates who descend into savery after being trapped in a mansion; suicide and violence and nightmares ensue, including the director's trademark trope of an animated severed hand.

CAPE FEAR
Production: USA, 1962
Director: J. Lee Thompson
Category: Crime Noir
One of Mitchum's best film noir vehicles, in which he follows his turn as a psychopath in **Night Of The Hunter** with another violent and dangerous character, the ex-convict Max Cady. Martin Scorsese directed an entetaining but grotesquely exaggerated remake in 1991, starring Robert de Niro as an over-the-top, biblical, almost superhuman Cady.

LA COMMARE SECCA
("The Grim Reaper")
Production: Italy, 1962
Director: Bernardo Bertolucci
Category: Murder
Bertolucci's debut remains one of his best. With a script by Pier Paolo Pasolini, the film centres around the murder of a prostitute, a mystery which Bertolucci tries to unveil through the testimony of multiple witnesses. With his next film, **Prima Della Rivoluzione**, the young director would truly explode onto the international scene.

CONFESSIONS OF AN OPIUM EATER
Production: USA, 1962
Director: Albert Zugsmith
Category: Drugs
Vincent Price is a sailor who falls into the clutches of Chinese drug-pushers. Exploitation, mostly unrelated to Thomas De Quincey's original book, but full of sleazy imagery. Zugsmith was something of a pulp visionary, producing Orson Welles' **Touch Of Evil** before progressing to his own projects. He made the even more bizarre drug movie **The Chinese Room** in 1966, thereby reaching the pinnacle of his twisted craft.

DOCTOR CRIPPEN
Production: UK, 1962
Director: Robert Lynn
Category: Murder

Hawley Harvey Crippen was an American physician hanged in Pentonville Prison in London on 23 November 1910, for the murder of his wife, Cora. Crippen and Cora had moved to England in 1900; at the time of his wife's sudden disppearence, he was known to have a secret lover. They were arrested trying to flee the country, and his wife's remains, almost totally dissolved in acid, were discovered beneath the floorboards of their rented house. Robert Lynn's **Doctor Crippen**, with Donald Pleasance in the title role, is a rather dry and stagey telling of the tale, with its only *frisson* of horror deriving from the grisly disposal of the corpse, but distinguished by the cinematography of Nicolas Roeg.

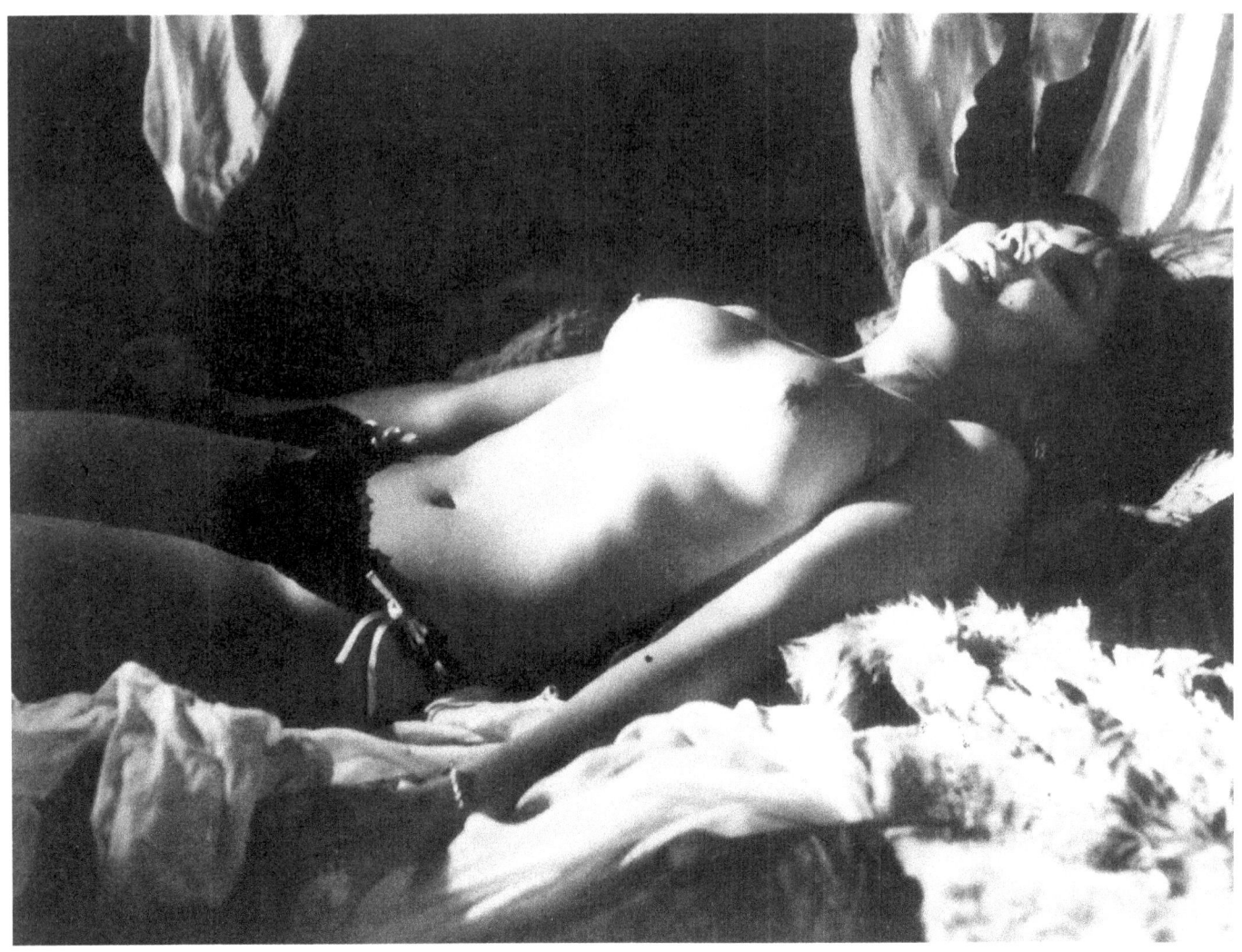

LA MANO DE UN HOMBRE MUERTO
("The Hand Of A Dead Man")
Production: Spain/France, 1962
Director: Jésus Franco
US release title: **The Sadistic Baron Von Klaus**
Category: Mayhem
Straddling the *krimi*, horror, and sexploitation genres, Franco's lurid tale of an aristocratic serial killer was censored in his native Spain upon release, but French versions retained its scenes of nudity, bondage and sadism.

MONDO CANE
("Dog's World")
Production: Italy, 1962
Director: Gualtiero Jacopetti, Franco Prosperi & Paolo Cavara
Category: Mondo

The film that gave its name to a whole genre of cinema – the mondo movie. With **Magia Verde** and others back in 1953, Italian film-makers had begun a line of "exotic doumentaries", sometimes part fabricated or staged, investigating weird wildlife, cultural practices and rites from around the world. With **Europa Di Notte** in 1958, this type of cinema also began to turn its attention closer to home and focus in on more sexual matters, and these two voyeuristic strands – definitively brought together in **Mondo Cane** – would form the fabric of the genre. In 1963 Jacopetti, Prosperi and Cavara followed up with the even more outrageous **Mondo Cane 2**, as well as **La Donna Nel Mondo** (mostly comprising out-takes from **Mondo Cane**), while Cavara went solo with **Malamondo** in 1964, presenting scenes of hog-butchery, nude skiing, and an orgy in a graveyard. By that time the "mondo" craze had well and truly exploded in Italy and beyond; Italian mondo films of this period include **Mondo Infame** (Roberto Bianchi Montero, 1963), **I Tabù** (Romolo Marcellini, 1963), **Mondo Matto Al Neon** (Carlo Veo, 1963), **Nude Per Vivere** (Elio Petri, Giuliano Montaldo, Giulio Questi, 1963), **Questo Mondo Proibito** (Frabizio

Gabella, 1963), **Le Città Proibite** (Giuseppe Maria Scotese, 1963), **Africa Sexy** (Roberto Bianchi Montero, 1963), **Ecco** (Gianni Proia, 1963), **Universo Proibito** (Roberto Bianchi Montero, 1963), **Mondo Nudo** (Francesco De Feo, 1963), **I Piaceri Del Mondo** (Vinicio Marinucci, 1963), **Le Schiave Esistono Ancora** (Maleno Malenotti, Roberto Malenotti, Folco Quilici, 1964), **Europa: Operazione Streep-Tease** (Renzo Russo, 1964), **Mondo Balordo** (Roberto Bianchi Montero, 1964), **Il Pelo Nel Mondo** (Marco Vicario, Antonio Margheriti, 1964), **Il Piacere E Il Mistero** (Enzo Peri, 1964), and **Donne Calde Di Notte** (Guy Perol, Sigmund Larsen, 1964).

NOZ W WODZIE
("Knife In The Water")
Production: Poland, 1962
Director: Roman Polanski
Category: Psycho
A twist on the "psychopath hitch-hitcher" trope, staged upon a boat out at sea and infused with high sexual tension. Ottavio Alessi's **Top Sensation** (1969) took elements from Polanski's film, whilst Ruggero Deodato's **Una Ondata Di Piacere** (1975) was a sleazy modification of the same plot; Phillip Noice's later **Dead Calm** (1989) upped the psycho-horror quotient of a similar onboard scenario.

LE PROCÈS
("The Trial")
Production: France/Italy/Germany/Yugoslavia, 1962
Director: Orson Welles
Category: Absurdism
Welles' adaptation of the seminal Kafka novel *Der Prozess* is his last great film, and the only great one he made after his excoriating masterpiece **Touch Of Evil**. Bleak and baroque, the film presents the world of men as a labyrinthine industrial maze of dead ends and nightmarish slatted non-sequiturs, all filmed from garishly extreme angles and lit like the most pessimistic of film noir damnations. Not content, Welles then perversely adds a final touch of his own in a dismissive, apocalyptic coda.

DER ROTE RAUSCH
("The Red Noise")
Production: Germany, 1962
Director: Wolfgang Schlief
Category: Krimi

Existential crime movie with Klaus Kinski in his first starring role as an obsessive, psychopathic woman-killer on the run from the insane asylum. Haunted and hunted by his own demons, Kinski's character seeks redemption but, finally, surrenders himself back to the mental ward. Kinski's presence in this film was a link to the popular Rialto/Edgar Wallace *gruselkrimis* of that period, but there is actually little similarity; while the Rialto films were gothic evocations of classic mystery and horror, **Der Rote Rausch** looks forward to the German New Wave in its austerity and psychological authenticity.

SAFETYBELT FOR SUSIE
Production: USA, 1962
Director: Pat Shields
Category: Driver Education
Driver safety film produced by Charles Cahill in association with the Institute of Traffic and Transportation Engineering at UCLA, designed to illustrate why everybody should buckle up. Massively violent footage of test-crash dummies being utterly demolished in high-speed collisions is the main feature of the film, a vivid simulacrum of high-velocity mayhem.

LE SEPTIÈME JURÉ
("The Seventh Juror")
Production: France, 1962
Director: Geoges Lautner
Category: Crime And Punishment
A prime example of female nudity in a mainstream crime drama, something only permitted in Europe at that time. The film concerns a middle-aged man who comes acaross a woman sun-bathing topless in a forest, is overcome by lust, and ends up killing her after an attempted rape.

DER TEPPICH DES GRAUENS
("Carpet Of Terror")
Production: Germany/Spain/Italy, 1962
Director: Harald Reinl
Category: Krimi

A German *gruselkrimi* in the macabre vein of the popular Rialto/Edgar Wallace films of that period, with Rialto/Wallace regulars Joachim Fuchsberger and Karin Dor, plus frequent director Harald Reinl. The story itself is certainly worthy of Wallace, and Reinl adds suitably macabre flourishes to this tale of an assassin who kills the rich using balls of poison gas.

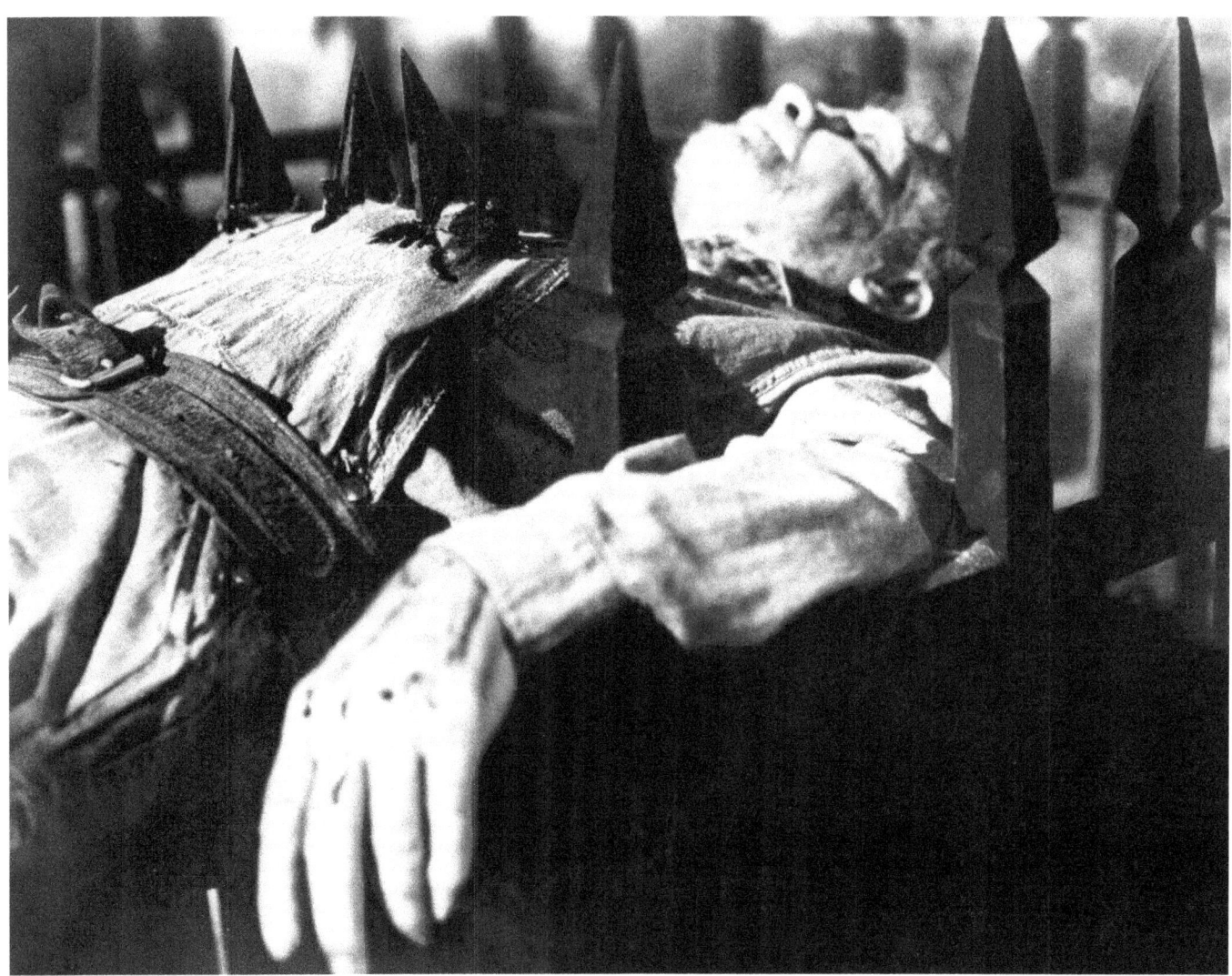

TERRIFIED
Production: USA, 1962
Director: Lew Landers
Category: Maniac

The last ever film by veteran director Landers was in the psycho-horror genre, the weird tale of a mask-wearing maniac who haunts an old ghost-town.

WHATEVER HAPPENED TO BABY JANE?
Production: USA, 1962
Director: Robert Aldrich
Category: Psychosis

An over-the-top grand guignolesque piece, with Bette Davis and Joan Crawford offering hideous self-parodies as two ageing sisters – one crippled, one crazy – who seemingly hate each other to the point of murder. On a par with Hitchcock's **Psycho** as a glimpse into the twilight world of the insane. The film even inspired a parodic homage from Italy, Ottavio Alessi's **Che Fine Ha Fatto Toto Baby?** ("Whatever Happened To Baby Toto?", 1964), concerning two criminal brothers who end up in a house of dope-smokers, go crazy, and commit a series of horrifyingly sadistic murders. Like Baby Jane, they end up in a lunatic asylum.

LA VENDETTA DI ERCOLE
("The Vengeance Of Hercules")
Production: Italy, 1960
Director: Vittorio Cottafavi
English release title: **Goliath And The Dragon**
Category: Myth/Peplum

MYTH

GLI AMORI DI ERCOLE
("The Loves Of Hercules")
Production: Italy, 1960
Director: Carlo Ludovico Bragaglia
English release title: **Hercules Vs. The Hydra**
Category: Myth/Peplum
Mickey Hargitay plays Hercules, with his wife Jayne Mansfield as Queen Deianira, one of the hero's "loves".

LA CAPERUCITA ROJA
("Red Riding Hood")
Production: Mexico, 1960
Director: Roberto Rodriguez
English release title: **Little Red Riding Hood**
Category: Fantasy

Attempted kids' movie is a surrealistic atrocity, suffused with an innate Mexican grotesquerie which makes it unsuitable for its target audience but affords some sick fascination for jaded adults. Promotional picture cards showed Little Red dressed like a barbecued hog and about to be carved up and devoured by a demented skunk and leering wolf, just one of the nightmarish images to be found in the film. Rodriguez followed up with the equally disturbing **Caperucita Y Sus Tres Amigos** (1961), and then topped it all off with the incredible **Caperucita Y Pulgarcito Contra Los Monstruos** (1962), a contorted fusion of grotesque fairy-tale and freak horror. At the dark heart of all three films the contorted figure of the dwarf Santanón can be found, hunched beneath a foetid skunk pelt. The best of Grimms' fairytales rank amongst the most grotesque, nightmarish and twisted in all literature; therefore, it follows that only films of the extreme imagination can fully do them justice. Others which have achieved this include Friz Freleng's beserk animation **Little Red Riding Rabbit** (1944), Matthew Bright's twisted psycho-road movie **Freeway** (1996), and Titus Moody's bizarre underground porno **Little Red Riding Hood** (1970), which depicts a wolf-masked intruder seducing both Red and her grandmother with drugs and an electric dildo. An earlier hardcore version of the story was the two-part stag movie **A Wolf's Story** aka **Wolfman** aka **Big Bad Wolf And Two Little Red Hoods That Rode** (1963-66).

DAI-BOSATSU TOGE
("Great Bodhisattva Pass")
Production: Japan, 1960
Director: Kenji Misumi
English release title: **Satan's Sword**
Category: Chambara

A classic sword-fight movie in two parts by Misumi (who would go on to direct episodes of **Zatoichi** and **Nemuri Kyoshiro**, as well as the best of the classic **Lone Wolf With Cub** series), based on *Daibosatsu-toge*, the traditional, picaresque story of Japanese heroism. Raizô Ichikawa stars as disturbed *samurai* Ryunosuke Tsukue. The trilogy was completed in 1961 by Kazuo Mori. Previous versions were filmed by Hiroshi Inagaki in 1935 and 1936, and by Tomu Ichida in 1957, 1958, and 1959. The best adaptation of all remains Kihachi Okamoto's annihilatory 1966 vision, released in English as **Sword Of Doom**, starring Tatsuya Nakadai (although it only tells the first part of the epic story).

FAUST

Production: Germany, 1960
Director: Peter Gorski, Gustaf Gründgens
Category: Myth

Out of the dozens of film versions of the Faust myth, this one in particular stands out as being worthy of mention in the same breath as Murnau's of 1926; the reason for this is that it is the only film record of Gustaf Gründgens' legendary portrayal of Mephistopheles. Gründgens had first played the role on stage back in 1932, and won universal acclaim for his mesmeric incarnation – so much so that his name became indelibly linked with that of the Devil. Finally, the actor agreed to return to the role in 1957, staging his own production, and the **Faust** of 1960 is a film record of that performance (which ran for two years), shot only a few years before the actor's death. Novelist Karl Mann based his 1936 book *Mephisto* on Gründgens' life, suggesting that the actor made his own infernal pact with the Nazis when he collaborated with their ascendent Third Reich; the story was filmed in 1980 by Hungarian director Istvan Szabo, as **Mephisto**, starring Klaus Maria Brandauer.

THE HELLFIRE CLUB
Production: UK, 1960
Director: Robert S. Baker, Monty Berman
Category: Historical

Baker and Berman were the borderline-exploitation team who produced various quasi-horror historical films in the 1950s and early 1960s. The Hellfire Club was a den of debauchery housed at Medmenham Abbey on the Thames around 1750, and presided over by Sir Francis Dashwood and other delinquent aristocrats. The motto *Fait ce que voudras* ("Do what thou wilt") was blazoned above a doorway in stained glass, and rumours abounded of Black Masses, orgies and Satan or demon worship within its walls. Unfortunately, the potentially interesting coupling of this legendary house of horror and the modern-day movie-makers never really comes off; apart from one very tame "orgy" sequence, **The Hellfire Club** largely plays itself out as a standard historical melodrama. However, shots of nude women and debauchery were restored for **Les Chevaliers Du Démon**, the French version of the film (it was common practice for Baker and Berman to shoot spicier scenes for their movies to be released for the European market). Perhaps Hammer would have handled the subject matter better, but the Baker-Berman attempt was to remain the only Hellfire Club film of the century (with the possible exception of **Hell Fire Club** [Climax In Color 2203], a European porno loop produced in the early 1970s).

MACISTE NELLA VALLE DEI RE
("Maciste In The Valley Of The Kings")
Production: Italy, 1960
Director: Carlo Campogalliani
English release title: **Son Of Samson**
Category: Myth/Peplum

The first in a series of modern Maciste films. Mark Forest, also seen as the bearded Ercole that year, plays Maciste. Many different actors would take the role over the following few years, as was the case with Italy's other main peplum characters. Forest next played Maciste in **Maciste, L'Uomo Più Forte Del Mondo** ("Maciste, The World's Strongest Man") in 1961, and the again in a sequel, **Maciste, Il Gladiatore Più Forte Del Mondo** ("Maciste, The World's Strongest Gladiator") in 1962.

LA RIVOLTA DEGLI SCHIAVI
("Revolt Of The Slaves")
Production: Italy, 1960
Director: Gianfranco Parolini
Category: Peplum
One of numerous Italian historical films which heavily featured gladitaors and the Roman arena.

URSUS

Production: Italy/Spain, 1960
Director: Carlo Campogalliani
Category: Peplum

The first film in Italy's Ursus series, starring Ed Fury in the title role. Spanish actress Soledad Miranda, best-known for softcore sex roles in Jess Franco movies, makes her credited film debut as a young sacrificial virgin. **Ursus** was released in 1961, as were the next two series entries **La Vendetta Di Ursus** and **Ursus E La Ragazza Tartara,** both with different actors. Fury would play Ursus twice more, and also Maciste in the anomalous **Maciste Contro Lo Sceicco** (1962).

ERCOLE AL CENTRO DELLA TERRA
("Hercules At the Centre Of The Earth")
Production: Italy, 1961
Director: Mario Bava
English release title: **Hercules In The Haunted World**
Category: Myth/Peplum
British body-builder Reg Park's second film appearance as Ercole (Hercules), who must enter the depths of Hades to destroy the evil King Lico (played by Christopher Lee). Visually rivalled only by Giorgio Ferroni's lavish depiction of Dionysus at Thebes, **Le Baccanti** (also 1961), and among the best of all peplums.

ERCOLE ALLA CONQUISTA DI ATLANTIDE
("Hercules And The Conquest Of Atlantis")
Production: Italy, 1961
Director: Vittorio Cottafavi
US release title: **Hercules And The Captive Women**
Category: Myth/Peplum
British body-builder Reg Park's first film appearance as Ercole (Hercules).

IL GIGANTE DI METROPOLIS
("The Titan Of Metropolis")
Production: Italy, 1961
Director: Umberto Scapelli
Category: Myth/Peplum
An unusual fusion of the peplum genre with outré SF elements, **Il Gigante Di Metropolis** plays out in the lost city of Atlantis, with set designs that recall Fritz

Lang's high-tech **Metropolis** fused with the pulp of **Flash Gordon** and the sacrificial grandeur of Aztec temples (the creation of Mario Bava's protégé Giorgio Giovannini). Gordon Mitchell plays the hero, who spends much of his time in bondage.

IL GLADIATORE INVINCIBILE
("The Invincible Gladiator")
Production: Italy, 1961
Director: Alberto De Martino
Category: Peplum

MACISTE CONTRO IL VAMPIRO
("Maciste Versus The Vampire")
Production: Italy, 1961
Director: Sergio Corbucci, Giacomo Gentilomo
English release title: **Goliath And The Vampires**
Category: Peplum/Horror

If the fusion of horror elements to the *peplum* genre was started by Mario Bava's **Ercole Al Centro Della Terra**, it was continued in this violent, darkly delirious entry, a year later. Gordon Scott stars as the legendary Maciste, pitted against a vampire lord and his legion of faceless minions. Another horror-tinged entry was **Maciste All'Inferno**, released in 1962 and starring Kirk Morris in the title role. Scott also played Maciste in Riccardo Freda's **Maciste Alla Corte Del Gran Khan** ("Maciste In The Court Of The Great Khan", also 1961).

SANSONE
("Samson")
Production: Italy, 1961
Director: Gianfranco Parolini
Category: Peplum

The first in Italy's Samson series, joining other mythic film strongmen like Ercole, Maciste, Ursus and Goliath. Brad Harris took the title role, a year after starring in the first in the Goliath series, **Goliath Contro I Giganti** ("Goliath vs. The Giants"). Serge Gainsbourg plays the villain, named Warkalla. He also played Hercules in **La Furia Di Ercole** (1962).

IL TRIONFO DI MACISTE
("The Triumph Of Maciste")
Production: Italy, 1961
Director: Tanio Boccia
Us release title: **Triumph Of The Son Of Hercules**.
Category: Peplum

The first appearance as Maciste by Kirk Morris. That same year the role was also played by Gordon Mitchell in **Maciste Nella Terra Dei Ciclopi** ("Maciste In The Land Of The Cyclops"), and by several other actors or body-builders. Morris next played Maciste in **Maciste All'Inferno** (1962).

YOJIMBO
("Defender")
Production: Japan, 1961
Director: Akita Kurosawa
Category: Chambara

Having produced a series of films in the 1950s which still stand as the pinnacle of the traditional samurai action movie, Kurosawa turned to the West with **Yojimbo**, based on the pulp novel *Red Harvest* by Dashiel Hammett (and possibly on Budd Boetticher's 1958 western **Buchanan Rides Out**), and played out in a setting easily recognisable from the American western. The plot – sword-slinging/gun-slinging stranger drifts into town and plays two warring factions against each other for his own gain – has since become cliché, but the film started an evolving, symbiotic triangulation between the *chambara* film, the American western and a new genre, the Italian "spaghetti" western, that lasted throughout the 1960s in terms of plots, action, violence, musical scores, and attitude. **Yojimbo** was remade by Sergio Leone as **Per Un Pugno Di Dollari**, and the rest is history. As well as the film's sardonic, existential tone, **Yojimbo** was notable for an increase in graphic violence – the brutal tone is established with an early shot of a dog with a severed hand in its mouth – a trend that Kurosawa continued in the loose sequel, **Sanjuro** (1962), where the "fountaining blood" effect that became a *chambara* staple was first introduced. Kurosawa directed **Akahige** in 1965 but, perhaps feeling he had taken the format to its limit, would not then return to the samurai film for almost fifteen years, producing **Kagemusha** in 1980, followed in 1985 by his crowning statement on the genre, **Ran;** his blueprint for a new, radical, blood-drenched *chambara* cinema in the 60s was instead taken up by new voices such as Kenji Misumi, Kihachi Okamoto, and Hideo Gosha.

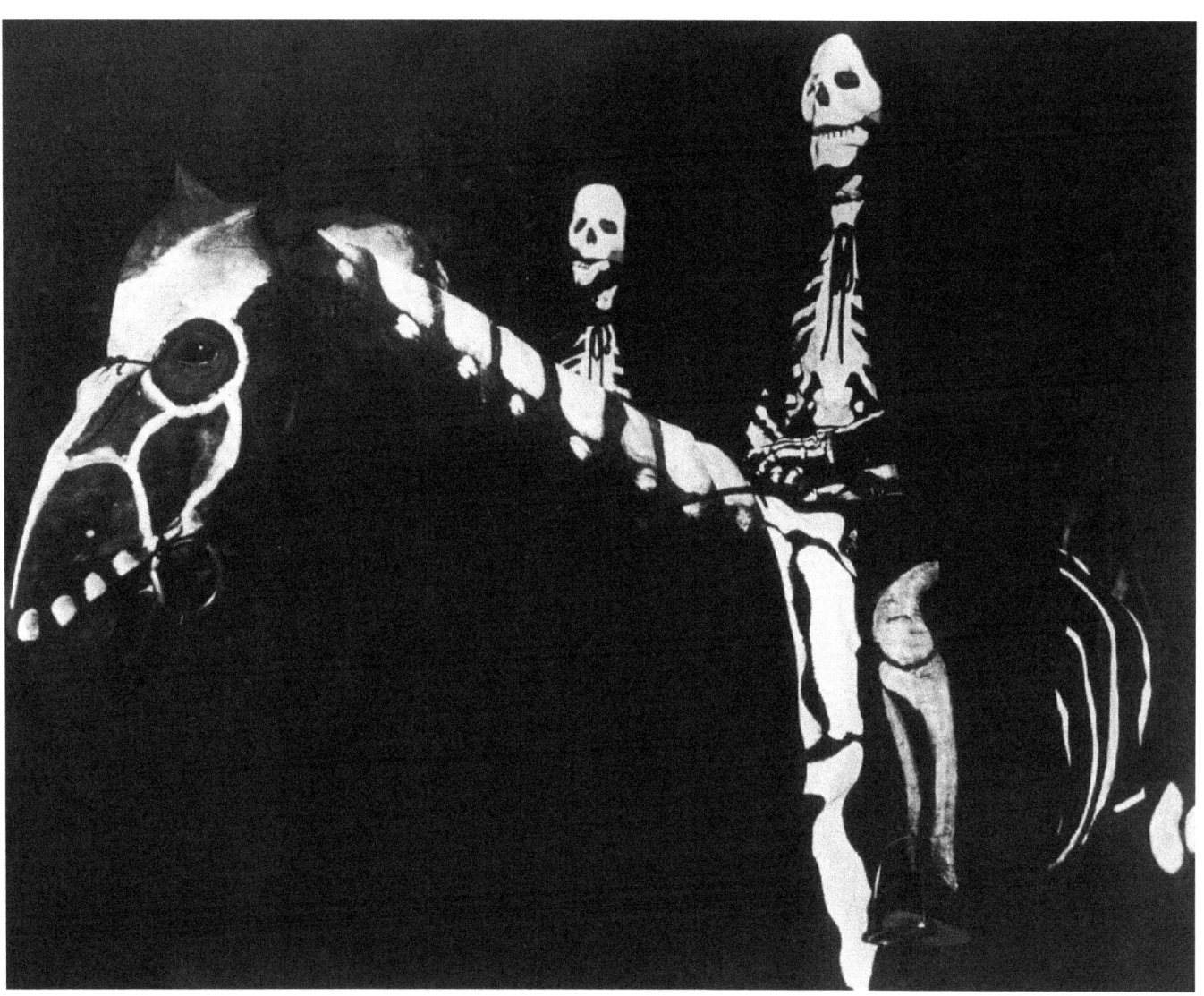

CAPTAIN CLEGG
Production: UK, 1962
Director: Peter Graham Scott
US release title: **Night Creatures**
Category: Pirates
Hammer Films' **Captain Clegg, The Pirates Of Blood River** (1962), and **The Devil-Ship Pirates** (1964) comprise a fine trilogy of period pirate movies. A young Oliver Reed makes stirring appearances in the first two, while Christopher Lee dominates both John Gilling's **Pirates Of Blood River** as cut-throat Laroche, and Don Sharp's

Devil-Ship Pirates as the merciless Captain Robeles. All three are marked by sadistic flourishes, but **Captain Clegg** is probably the most interesting, being the most horrific and inventive, and involves smuggling in the Romney marshes by the notorious rum-runner Clegg (Peter Cushing) and his men, the Marsh Phantoms. Dressed as hooded skeletons, they are capable of frightening an observer to death, disguising a look-out man as a scarecrow, conveying contraband whisky in hearses, cutting out the tongues of traitors, and otherwise lending a grotesque air to the rural night.

DAUGHTER OF THE SUN GOD
Production: USA, 1962
Director: Kenneth Hartford
Category: Jungle Fantasy

EEGAH
Production: USA, 1962
Director: Arch Hall Sr.
Category: Fantasy

IL FIGLIO DI SPARTACUS
("Son Of Spartacus")
Production: Italy, 1962
Director: Sergio Corbucci
English release title: **The Slave**
Category: Peplum
Perhaps the stand-out of the gladiator films released in 1962, given the presence of original Hercules actor Steve Reeves. Others in the same vein included **Il Gladiatore Di Roma, Solo Contro Roma,** and the Italian/Spanish co-production **I Sette Gladiatori.**

MACISTE ALL'INFERNO
("Maciste In Hell")
Production: Italy, 1962
Director: Riccardo Freda
English release title: **The Witch's Curse**
Category: Peplum/Horror

MACISTE CONTRO I MOSTRI
("Maciste Vs. The Monsters")
Production: Italy/Yugoslavia, 1962
Director: Guido Malatesta
Category: Peplum/Horror
A one-off Maciste adventure starring Reg Lewis, and featuring various monsters which terrorize two warring primitive tribes.

EL RAPTO DE LAS SABINAS
("The Rape Of The Sabine Women")
Production: Mexico, 1962
Director: Alberto Gout
Category: Myth/Peplum
Mexico also joined the peplum craze, notably with this exploitational version of an ancient Roman atrocity myth.

SEPPUKU
("Ritual Suicide")
Production: Japan, 1962
Director: Masaki Kobayashi
Category: Chambara

SHINOBI NO MONO
("Ninja Story")
Production: Japan, 1962
Director: Satsuo Yamamoto
English release title: **Band Of Assassins**
Category: Ninja

Regarded as the most accurate screen portrayal of *ninjas* up to that time, based on a novel by Maruyama Kazuyoshi, and focusing on the 16th century *ninja*/outlaw Ishikawa Goemon, who in real life was captured and boiled alive in a vat of oil. Here Goemon is played by Raizo Ichikawa, and is shown being pursued by rival *ninjas* and carrying out ingenious assassinations. This was the film that launched a new wave of more realistic, adult *ninja* cinema which eschewed the magical adventure elements of earlier movies in favour of arcane and violent martial arts skills, shadow-bound espionage, and grim fatalism. Director Yamamoto followed up with the action-packed sequel **Zoku Shinobi no Mono** in 1963; other notable genre entries, all shot in scintillant black-and-white, include Yatsuo Hasegawa's **Jushichinin no Ninja** (1963), Tetsuya Yamaguchi's **Ninja Gari** (1964), Kono Toshikazu's **Daisan No Ninja** (1964), and, most complex of all, Masahiro Shinoda's **Ibun Sarutobi Sasuke** (1965).

ULISSE CONTRO ERCOLE
("Ulysses Versus Hercules")
Production: Italy, 1962
Director: Mario Caiano
Category: Myth/Peplum

URSUS GLADIATORE RIBELLE
("Ursus, Rebel Gladiator")
Production: Italy, 1962
Director: Domenico Paolella
English release title: **Rebel Gladiators**
Category: Peplum
One of two Ursus films produced in 1962; the other was **Ursus Nella Valle Dei Leoni** ("Ursus In The Valley Of Lions"), with original actor Ed Fury.

VAXDOCKAN
("The Wax Doll")
Production: Sweden, 1962
Director: Arne Mattsson
Category: Fantasy

ZATOICHI MONOGATARI
("The Story Of Zatoichi")
Production: Japan, 1962
Director: Kenji Misumi
Category: Chambara

The first entry in one of Japan's longest-running film series, which continued for a further 24 entries until 1973. All the films starred Shintaro Katsu as Zatoichi, a blind monk adept at martial arts and combat. This was followed by **Zoku Zatoichi Monogatari,** also in 1962, directed by Kazuo Mori. Both films were shot in black and white.

THE TIME MACHINE
Production: USA, 1960
Director: George Pal
Category: Science Fiction

SCI-FI

BEYOND THE TIME BARRIER
Production: USA, 1960
Director: Edgar G. Ulmer
Category: Science Fiction

NEUTRÓN, EL ENMASCARADO NEGRO
("Neutron, The Man In The Black Mask")
Production: Mexico, 1960
Director: Federico Curiel
Category: Science Fiction/Wrestling
The first of three pulp SF films from 1960 starring Wolf Ruvinskis as wrestler Neutron, who fights an evil scientist and his lethal army of automata. The other two films were **Los Autómatas De La Muerte** and **Neutrón Contra El Doctor Caronte**.

DER SCHWEIGENDE STERN
("The Silent Star")
Production: East Germany/Poland, 1960
Director: Kurt Naetzig
US release title: **First Spaceship To Venus**
Category: Science Fiction
This allegory on nuclear proliferation was one of a very few influential SF films to emerge from the Eastern Bloc. The wreckage of an alien spacecraft is found in Siberia, and is found to be from Venus. Earth cosmonauts set out to make contact, only discovering along the way that the Venusians were planning to devastate the planet with nuclear warheads. The set designs, especially the bizarre alien landscapes of Venus, are brilliantly realised, and the film also carries significant philosophical weight. It was originally released in the USA in a butchered version titled **First Spaceship To Venus,** with lots of footage cut out. From a novel by Stanislaw Lem, author of *Solaris*.

SPACE-MEN

Production: Italy/Japan, 1960
Director: Antonio Margheriti
US release title: **Assignment Outer Space**
Category: Science Fiction

An early example of Margheriti's ability to conjure up intriguing visions on a small budget, a skill which would hold him in good stead for his long career in genre movies. Shame the plot – about averting a malfunctioning spaceship from hurtling to Earth – is so boring. **Space-Men** was Margheriti's first SF film; his second was **Il Pianeta Degli Uomini Spenti** (1961).

VILLAGE OF THE DAMNED
Production: UK, 1960
Director: Wolf Rilla
Category: Science Fiction
An adaptation of John Wyndham's novel *The Midwich Cuckoos*, concerning a mass immaculate conception which leads to the birth of telepathic alien children. A sequel of sorts, **Children Of The Damned,** appeared in 1963, concerning six ESP-gifted children and the fearful authorities' endeavours to hunt them down and exterminate them.

THE AVENGERS
Production: UK, 1961-69
Director: Various
Category: Science Fiction/Spy
The most stylish British TV production of all time, a secret agent vehicle with strong science fictional elements which ran to seven series. Patrick Macnee, as John Steed, was the one constant in the show, which saw him partnered first by a Dr Keel, and then in subsequent series by three different sexy female partners: Cathy Gale (Honor Blackman), Emma Peel (Diana Rigg), and Tara King (Linda Thorson). As the series progressed the stories became more and more outré and surrealistic, peaking with the second two seasons featuring Rigg and the first (and only) with Thorson. Many episodes featured the very best British directors, screenwriters and supporting actors; stand-outs include: "The Winged Avenger", "The Joker", "Return Of The Cybernauts", "Epic", "The Forget-Me-Knot", "Game", and the grand finale, "Bizarre". The franchise was briefly revived in the 70s, but the results were a best-forgotten travesty. An ill-considered Hollywood film version in 1998 was even more pathetic.

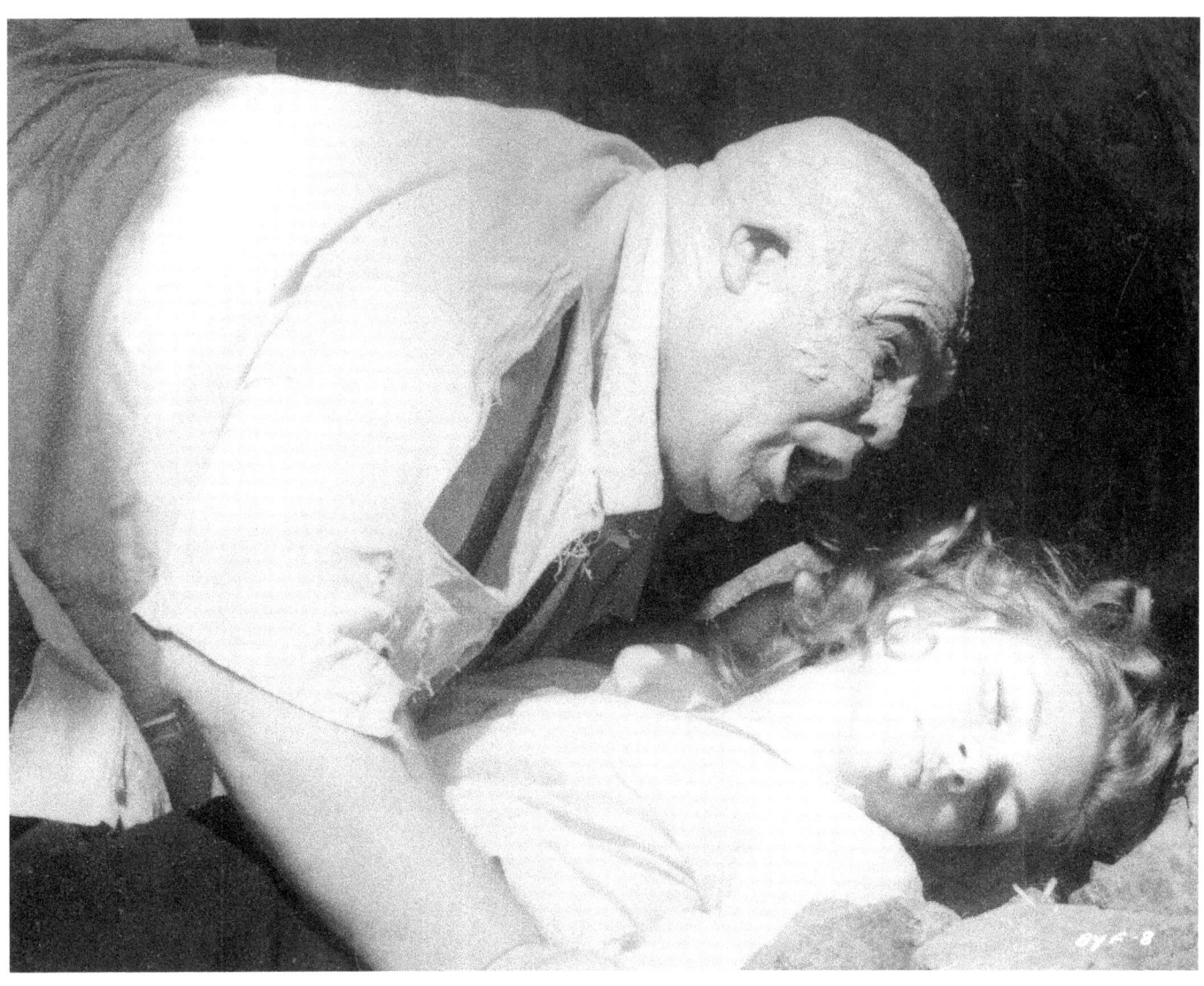

BEAST OF YUCCA FLATS
Production: USA, 1961
Director: Coleman Francis
Category: Science Fiction

Wrestler Tor Johnson plays an atomic scientist blasted by a nuclear explosion and chased by sinister agents. He hides out in a cave with a rabbit, grabs women, and licks their hair. The film has little dialogue, prefering to use an off-screen narrator who delivers strange quasi-philosophical blurbs which only serve to double the on-screen confusion. A juddering elipse of discordant non-cinema.

CREATURE FROM THE HAUNTED SEA
Production: USA, 1961
Director: Roger Corman
Category: Science Fiction

THE DAMNED

Production: UK, 1961
Director: Joseph Losey
Category: Science Fiction

Hammer's best entry into the SF arena, boasting no less a talent than Joseph Losey as director, was an extremely problematic venture for the company. From the starting-point of H.L. Lawrence's tale *The Children Of Light*, Losey and writer Evan Jones had fashioned an intellectually chilling story of a group of children reared in an artificial, radioactive world to enable them to survive in the aftermath of a nuclear war; set in a British coastal resort, the plot also featured a vicious gang of motorcycle thugs (led by Oliver Reed, outstanding in one of his nine early appearances for Hammer), whose sadism was extreme for the time. The final screenplay was so far removed from Hammer's original concept that the collaboration became fraught from the outset; the film was cut before release (even more drastically so in America) and held on the shelf for a good two years. Losey's apparent aim was to make the ultimate statement in the cycle of apocalyptic SF films which had started in the 50s. Photographed with sombre brilliance by Arthur Grant, the result was a bleak, downbeat work whose ending proffers little hope. MacDonald Carey plays an American businessman whose interest in a young woman (Shirley Ann Field) results in his beating at the hands of King (Reed), her incestuously over-protective brother. He finally uncovers the government child-breeding scheme, which is overseen by the cold figure of Bernard (Alexander Knox), whose former lover (Viveca Lindfors) is terminally disturbed and spends her time creating hideous, mutant sculptures. Losey draws all the strands of the story together with his customary skill, transcending the nastiness of the material, and leaves us with a frighteningly plausible, nihilistic climax in which Carey, Field and the cycle gang attempt to liberate the irradiated children but are savagely put down by cold, institutionalised violence. The film's themes have been taken up many times since, but Losey's vision of totalitarian atrocity has perhaps yet to be surpassed in its disturbing intensity. An adaptation of John Wyndham, **Village Of The Damned** (from his novel *The Midwich Cuckoos*), was made the same year, but the films are unconnected despite the title similarity and both having a plot about weird children. Losey's first credited (under his own name) UK film, the bizarre crime short **A Man On The Beach** (1955), was also directed for Hammer.

THE DAY THE EARTH CAUGHT FIRE
Production: UK, 1961
Director: Val Guest
Category: Science Fiction

An apocalyptic SF movie, and one of the best in that genre; two simultaneous nuclear test blasts in different parts of the world knock the planet off its orbit and spinning towards the sun, causing masive heat waves, droughts, and enforced water rationing. As time begins to run out, another massive detonation is arranged, the only hope of putting the earth back in its proper orbit. The film ends with this explosion; we never discover the outcome (an unusually uncomforting finale for a movie of that period). Until later directors of similar films, director Guest largely eschews special effects to focus on what happens to human relationships when complete destruction is imminent. As a telescoping of global warming, the film still has enormous relevance

GORGO
Production: UK, 1961
Director: Eugène Lourié
Category: Science Fiction

KONGA
Production: UK, 1961
Director: John Lemont
Category: Science Fiction/Fantasy

LA MARCA DEL MUERTO
("The Mark Of The Dead Man")
Production: Mexico, 1961
Director: Fernando Cortés
Category: Science Fiction/Horror

THE MOST DANGEROUS MAN ALIVE
Production: USA, 1961
Director: Allan dwan
Category: Science Fiction
B-director Dwan brings a certain pulp poetry to this fierce SF tale of a gangster whose flesh turns to steel.

MOSURA

Production: Japan, 1961
Director: Ishiro Honda
English release title: **Mothra**
Category: Science Fiction

One of the best in Honda/Toho's series of *daikaiju* movies, featuring a gigantic moth. The end of Mothra's larval stage is perhaps the most impressive sequence, with some psychedelic cumshots as a giant phallic worm spurts white cocoon fabric high into the Tokyo night.

PHANTOM PLANET
Production: USA, 1961
Director: William Bernds
Category: Science Fiction

IL PIANETA DEGLI UOMINI SPENTI
("Planet Of Dead Men")
Production: Italy, 1961
Director: Antonio Margheriti
English release title: **Battle Of The Worlds**
Category: Science Fiction
Margheriti's second (and maybe best early) SF movie, and the third ever from Italy, depicts the Earth under attack from aliens. A battle with spacecraft ensues, one of the first ever attempts at showing this kind of dogfight in outer space.

REPTILICUS
Production: Denmark/USA, 1961
Director: Poul Bang
Category: Science Fiction

CHELOVEK-AMFIBIYA
("Amphibian Man")
Production: USSR, 1962
Director: Vladimir Chebotaryov, Gennadi Kazansky
Category: Science Fiction
A very unusual Russian SF film, concerning a young man who has a shark's gills implanted in his neck so he can live underwater. Although at first believed by locals to be a sea-devil, it turns out his purpose is more benign – he was designed to be the prototype for a new race of amphibious humans living in a Utopian underwater republic. From a novel by SF writer Alexander Belyaev.

CREATION OF THE HUMANOIDS
Production: USA, 1962
Director: Wesley Barry
Category: Science Fiction

THE DAY MARS INVADED EARTH
Production: USA, 1962
Director: Maury Dexter
Category: Science Fiction

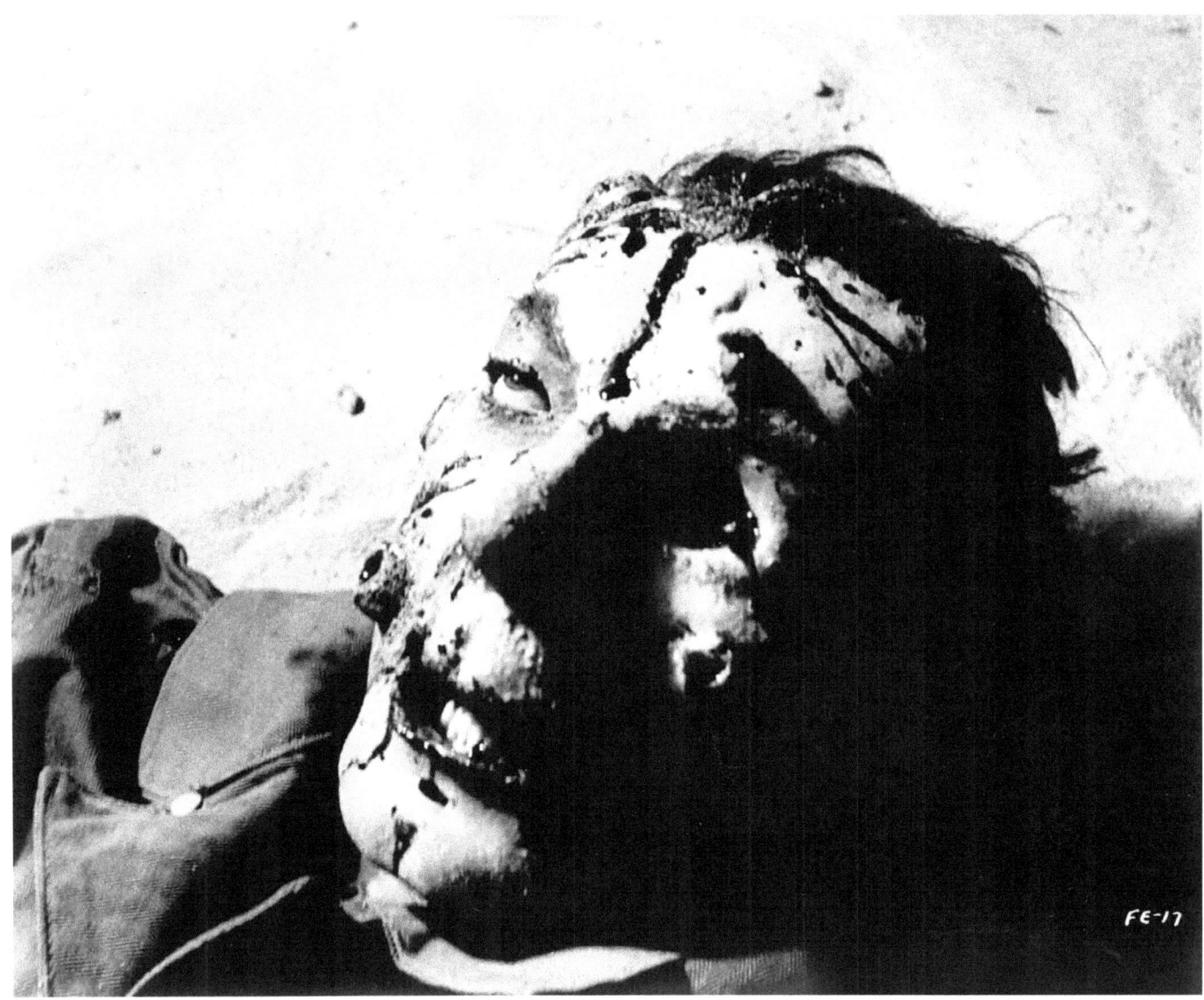

THE FLESH EATERS
Production: USA, 1962/64
Director: Jack Curtis
Category: Science Fiction/Horror
Nazi experiments create a breed of sea-slugs which feed on human flesh. The film is notable for its fairly extreme gore effects, which actually pre-date those of Herschell Gordon Lewis' **Blood Feast** in terms of production (but not release). Bodies stripped to the bloody bone, eyeball destruction, and evisceration are amongst the crude scenes of carnage.

INVASION OF THE STAR CREATURES
Production: USA, 1962
Director: Bruno Ve Sota
Category: Science Fiction
"Beautiful... deadly... in their veins the blood of monsters!" Sex-starved alien females are seduced and tamed by Earth soldiers. Director Ve Sota was a veteran actor of bizarre movies, such as **Dementia** and **The Undead**.

LA JETÉE
("The Jetty")
Production: France, 1962
Director: Chris Marker
Category: Science Fiction

JOURNEY TO THE SEVENTH PLANET
Production: Denmark/USA, 1962
Director: Sid Pink
Category: Science Fiction

OTOSHIANA
("Pitfall")
Production: Japan, 1962
Director: Hiroshi Teshigahara
Category: Science Fiction

At the most sublime end of the science fiction movie scale are the symbolistic collaborations between the writer Kobo Abe and director Hiroshi Teshigahara, of which **Otoshiana** was the first. Abe, whose novels feature Ballardian notions of identity implosion and the zoning of inner space to postulate the human body/psyche itself as ultimate event horizon, also wrote the screenplays for Teshigahara's film adaptations. Later Abe/Teshigahara collaborations would include **Suna No Onna** (1964), **Tanin No Kao** (1967), and **Moetsukita Chizu** (1968).

PANIC IN THE YEAR ZERO
Production: USA, 1962
Director: Ray Milland
Category: Science Fiction

An artless addition to the genre of nuclear destruction movies, with director Milland also starring as man who, fully prepared for the sneak atomic attack that

hits Los Angeles, takes his family up into the hills where his survivalist training is put into ruthless practice. A grim, dog-eat-dog scenario which would be echoed in many subsequent movies dealing with a post-apocalyptic breakdown of society and moral codes.

PLANETA BUR
("Storm Planet")
Production: USSR, 1962
Director: Pavel Klushantsev
Category: Science Fiction

With **Planeta Bur**, Pavel Klushantsev pioneered and invented legendary special effects techniques for filming the planets, stars and weightnessless. He virtually redefined the science fiction genre, profoundly influencing the way Hollywood made SF films as the 1960s progressed. Roger Corman bought the rights to this movie and twice used it as the basis for hack abortions: Curtis Harrington's **Voyage To The Prehistoric Planet** and Peter Bogdanovich's **Voyage To The Planet Of Prehistoric Women,** thereby dragging it back to the camp 50s arena it had originally eclipsed. Always involved with the Soviet space program, Klushantsev's last films were **Luna** (1965) and **Mars** (1968).

FLITTERWOCHEN IN DER HÖLLE
("Honeymoon In Hell")
Production: Germany, 1960
Director: Johannes Kai
US release title: **Isle Of Sin**
Category: Sexploitation/Crime

SEX

THE ADVENTURES OF LUCKY PIERRE
Production: USA, 1960
Director: Herschell Gordon Lewis
Category: Nudie-Cutie

Before inventing the ultra-gore genre with **Blood Feast,** Lewis started out directing "nudie-cutie" flicks, and this was his first – and also the first of its type in colour, following the success of Russ Meyer's monochrome **The Immoral Mr. Teas** in 1959. A series of saucy vignettes shows Pierre encountering various unclothed ladies, including one segment set in a children's playground. Lewis had previously made two films (**The Prime Time** and **Living Venus**) with flashes of female nudity (including a naked swim scene by Karen Black, in her screen debut), but this was his wholesale plunge into the flesh market.

COLLEGE CONFIDENTIAL
Production: USA, 1960
Director: Albert Zugsmith
Category: Sexploitation

Teen sex exploitation as a college professor monitors the sexual habits of his students. Mamie Van Doren steals the show, as ever. Zugsmith, a top predator, also made **Sex Kittens Go To College** and **The Private Lives Of Adam And Eve** with Van

Doren the same year. These comedic films were as daring as times would permit within the Hollywood mainstream of domestic cinema; more explicit offerings such as nudie-cuties were as yet confined to more underground producers and exhibition circuits, or indeed Europe where the release version of **Sex Kittens Go To College** included an additional 9-minute dream sequence with four strippers.

FIEND OF DOPE ISLAND
Production: USA, 1960
Director: Nate Watt
Category: Sexploitation

FORM MISTRESS
Production: UK, c.1960
Director: Anonymous
Category: Sex/Adult

The box cover of this 200-foot, 8mm black-and-white "glamour" film for home projection and "adult viewing only" carries a drawing of a bare-breasted young woman poised by a school blackboard, indicating its content. Other reels from the same producer/distributor, Express, include **Daughter Of The Sun**, **Private Party**, **Playtime Girl**, and **River Nudes**. It is likely that topless nudity was the most these commercially-sold films had to offer to their slavering clientele; in the UK, harder material could only be found under the counter in Soho and other daring vice zones.

MANY WAYS TO SIN
Production: USA, 1960
Director: J.G. Tiger
Category: Sexploitation

This early sexploitation film is now believed lost, but an extant poster produced by William Mishkin Distribution promises the viewer "13 sinners", with salacious images each attributed to a particular transgression including lust, sensuality, depravity, seduction, and immorality.

NUDE ON THE MOON
Production: USA, 1960
Director: Doris Wishman
Category: Nudie/Science Fiction

Two astronauts land of the moon, only to find it populated by naked women (with antennae). The first, and most ludicrous, nudie-cutie directed by Doris Wishman (although she had also worked, uncredited, on Larry Wolk's **Hideout In The Sun** from the same year). Wishman would go on to be one of the queens of sexploitation cinema in the 60s; her other nudist films included **Diary Of A Nudist, Gentlemen Prefer Nature Girls,** and **Behind The Nudist Curtain,** but her distinctive, almost avant-garde style of presenting sordid sex reveries first came to the surface with **The Sex Perils Of Paulette** and **Bad Girls Go To Hell,** both from 1965. Amongst other early US nudist films of note were Joel Halt's **The Shameless,** Dick Crane's **Mr Peter's Pets,** Manuel Conde's **Girls On The Rocks,** Francis Ford Coppola's **Tonight For Sure,** and Ted V. Mikels' **Doctor Sex.** By 1964/65, the naturist format had twisted into sub-sub-genres like the "horror-nudie" (Ferenc Leroget's **Monster Of Camp Sunshine,** Barry Mahon's **The Beast That Killed Women**), a sure sign it was dying out; this period saw the first films in two new, darker sex regimes, the "roughie" and the "kinkie". Ray Phelan, cinematographer for **Nude On The Moon,** went on to direct **Too Young, Too Immoral** (1962), a trashy drugsploitation movie with future Warhol star Taylor Mead as a deaf-mute drug dealer who gets hurled from a speeding subway train, followed by **Assignment: Female** in 1965.

LA VÉRITÉ
("The Truth")
Production: France, 1960
Director: Henri-Georges Clouzot
Category: Sex/Murder

AMOURS CÉLÈBRES
("Famous Loves")
Production: France, 1961
Director: Michel Boisrond
Category: Sexploitation

LA BRIDE SUR LE COU
("Bridle On The Neck")
Production: France, 1961
Director: Roger Vadim, Jean Aurel
Category: Sex Comedy

CELLMATES

Production: USA, c.1961
Director: Anonymous
Category: Homo-Erotic

A queer men-in-prison loop from Zenith, a pioneering production company in the field of homoerotic cinema formed by Richard Fontaine around 1953 with films such as **The Vice And The Badge** (aka **Beach Bar Nightmare**), an 18-minute fantasy with male nudity. Fontaine also released films under the names MidWest Films and R.A. Enterprises, apparently to give an impression of competition. Originally filming in only in 16mm sound, Fontaine later made 8mm versions available to the private sales market. These productions were the first theatrically released homoerotic films. **Cellmates** follows the general Zenith formula: the film shows two male prisoners stripping naked, sitting on each other's legs to perform sit-ups, kissing, and finally lying down together. There is no explicit sexual activity or frontal nudity. Fontaine also worked with Bob Mizer, whose AMG company produced **Boys In Prison** and **Jailhouse Rumble** (both c.1960) in the same genre. Zenith films adopted racier titles as the 60s progressed (such as **Hustler And Prostitute Perversion** from 1966), but ceased production around 1970, as Fontaine seemed reluctant to enter the burgeoning world of explict sex movies – among which was **Jail House Rock** (Bob Anthony Studio, 1969), in which two male convicts with "10-inch cocks" (Joe Markum and Steve Ahern) fuck and suck each other. Other explicit MIP loops were **Cellblock** (Falcon, c.1973), **Prison Sex** (Golden Press, 1974), **Jail Bait** (BAS, 1975), and the two-reel **Cell Block** (1976) from Griffin International, in which a male prisoner is sexually brutalized in his cell by a gun-wielding, leather-clad motorcycle cop. A longer work was the 40-minute **Inmates** (Rollo Productions, 1973). Pre-condom men-in-prison hardcore features of note include **Prison For Life** (1977) and **Cell Block #9** (Joe Gage, 1981).

COMMON LAW WIFE

Production: USA, 1961
Director: Larry Buchanan
Category: Sexploitation

A hillbilly drive-in classic, in which stripper Baby Doll moves back to the bayou to shack up with her Uncle Shug when he strikes it rich. Trouble arises when Shug's common law wife refuses to move out, and meanwhile Baby Doll runs wild with a sex spree in the swamps. Buchanan followed up with **Free, White And 21**, an examination of racial tensions in the South with a black businessman on trial for rape. Sadly, the director soon got hired by AIP to make a series of cheap remakes of their 50s SF films, thereby curtailing his burgeoning career in exploitative but questioning backwoods psycho-dramas.

EROTICA
Production: USA, 1961
Director: Russ Meyer
Category: Nudie-Cutie
A nudie-movie comprising six separate vignettes, framed by a lecture on film-making; the episodes are: **Naked Innocence, Beauties, Bubbles And H2O, The Bear And The Bare, Nudists On The High Seas, The Nymphs**, and **The Bikini Busters**.

LEBENSBORN
("Fount Of Life")
Production: Germany, 1961
Director: Werner Klingler
US release title: **Ordered To Love**
Category: Sexploitation
An early example of Nazi sex exploitation, focusing on Hitler's *lebensborn* procreation program and its implied sexual atrocities. The US release boasted sleazy taglines such as "Teen-age girls forced to submit in secret Nazi mating camps" and "Hitler's depraved experiment in human breeding".

MALE AND FEMALE SINCE ADAM AND EVE
Production: Argentina, 1961
Director: Carlos Rinaldi
Category: Sexploitation

NAKED – AS NATURE INTENDED
Production: UK, 1961
Director: George Harrison Marks
Category: Nudism

First feature film by Harrison-Marks, previously a purveyor of Super-8 glamour reels for home consumption. **Naked – As Nature Intended** was one of the early glut of UK nudist films, and featured Pamela Green, the top glamour model in England at the time who can also be seen in Michael Powell's **Peeping Tom**.

THE RUINED BRUIN
Production: USA, 1961
Director: John K. McCarthy
Category: Nudiie-Cutie
The most bizarre of the nudie-cuties, concerning a bear who escapes from the zoo because he wants to be human. Mistaken for a man in costume at a nude pool party, he almost gets to fuck two girls in a pseudo-plushie/bestiality romp.

TROPICO DI NOTTE
("Night Tropic")
Production: Italy, 1961
Director: Renzo Russo
Category: Sexy Mondo
Very early "sexy nocturne" movie, a feature-length documentary showing ladies of the night in exotic locations. Russo quickly followed up with **Sexy** (1962) and **Mondo Calde Di Notte** (1962), two more examples of the voyeuristic genre that began with Alessandro Blasetti's **Europa Di Notte** in 1959 and continued with the likes of Luigi Vanzi's **Il Mondo di Notte** (1959), Gianni Proia's **Il Mondo di Notte Numero 2** (1961), Mino Loy's **Mondo Sexy Di Notte** (1962), Ettore Fecchi's **Sexy al Neon** (1962), and Pasquale De Fina's **Sexy ad alta Tensione** (1963).

WEST END JUNGLE
Production: UK, 1961
Director: Arnold L. Miller
Category: Sex Documentary
Perhaps the first British "mondo"-type film, a sex docmentary on London's vice zone Soho with all its strip clubs, massage parlours, dancers, hookers, pimps and punters. The film was actually made in response to the Wolfenden Street Offences Act of 1959, which removed prostitutes from the streets of London and drove them underground. Not surprisingly, **West End Jungle** was banned by the British censor. Miller went on to direct further vice exposés, in the form of **London In The Raw** (1964) and **Primitive London** (1965). Other additions to this small sub-genre of English cinema include Edward Stewart Abraham's **Our Incredible World** (1966) and Norman Cohen's **The London Nobody Knows**, from 1967.

AI
("Love")
Production: Japan, 1962
Director: Takahiko Iimura
Category: Sex/Underground
This seminal underground film, with a cacophonous soundtrack by Yoko Ono, is a catalogue of sex acts filmed at such close proximity that the sexual organs and

gasping mouths of the participants become indistinguishably blurred. A landmark of revolutionary Japanese cinema. Also in 1962, Iimura made **On Eye Rape** with Natsuyuki Nakanishi, derived from found sex education films. In response to the censored pubic hair in these films, Iimura inserted a still of one as a subliminal image and also punched holes into the film frames through the censored images, as if censoring censorship. Iimura was a prolific film-maker, whose other films of this period included **De Sade** (1962), a short (10 minutes) experimental film that utilizes 18th century lithographs to illustrate the Marquis de Sade and *120 Days Of Sodom*, set to erotic whispers, contemporary pop music and Michaut's *Notre-Dame Mass*, and **Onan** (1963), with disturbing images of a masturbating youth who gets off by burning and mutilating pictures of naked women.

BACHELOR TOM PEEPING
Production: USA, 1962
Director: Bill Dewar
Category: Nudiie-Cutie

BLAZE STARR GOES NUDIST
Production: USA, 1962
Director: Doris Wishman
Category: Nudism
One of the best-looking of Wishman's nudist camp films, before she progressed to sexploitation psychodramas. Starring super-stripper blaze Starr, who strips off to show her amazingly voluptuous figure at every opportunity. Too much filler in-between, but worth the wait. To see Blaze Starr in real action, check out the 1956 striptease compilation **Pin-Up Poses Of Blaze Starr**, in which she runs through some of her most famous routines, including "Screen Test" and "Dance Of Fire".

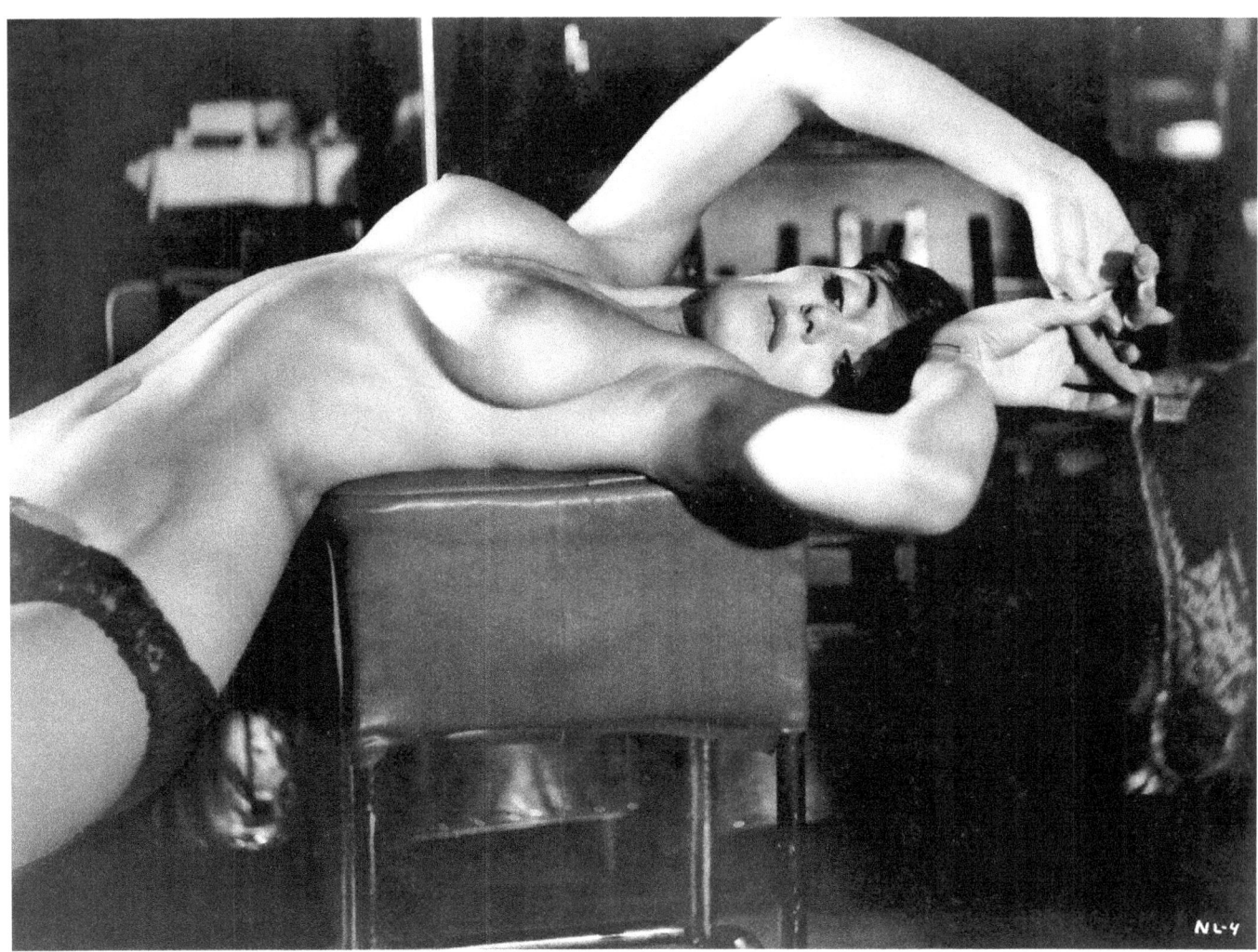

LE CONCERTO DE LA PEUR
("The Concerto Of Fear")
Production: France, 1962
Director: José Bénazéraf
Category: Sex/Crime
Bénazéraf's original French film, a typically languid meditation on the female form with a sub-plot about drug gangs and a Chet Baker free-jazz score, was bought by American producer Bob Cresse, who had his associate R. Lee Frost shoot some additional striptease scenes and then re-edited and over-dubbed it as **Night Of Lust**.

DAUGHTER OF THE SUN
Production: USA, 1962
Director: Herschell Gordon Lewis
Category: Nudism
The first film shot by Lewis in Florida, a thinly-plotted nudist colony movie starring the voluptuous and naked Rusty Allen. He quickly followed up with more of the same, **Nature's Playmates**, and carried on with, and experimented with, the nudie format for several more films, including **Goldilocks And The Three Bares** (1963 – a nudie-musical), and **Boin-n-g!** (1963 – a nudie-comedy). His last nudie was **Bell, Bare, And Beautiful** (1963), made just before he switched to horror with the landmark splatter movie **Blood Feast**.

LA DÉNONCIATION
("The Denunciation")
Production: France, 1962
Director: Jacques Doniol-Valcroze
Category: Murder
A notable example of female nudity being integrated into French mainstream cinema, something which in 1962 could not happen in countries such as the USA or the UK. It would be at least another seven years before it could.

HOUSE ON BARE MOUNTAIN
Production: USA, 1962
Director: Lee Frost, Wes Bishop
Category: Nudie-Cutie

Along with the likes of **Kiss Me Quick** and **Fanny Hill Meets Dr. Erotico**, this was a precursor of jokey nudie/sex/horror films such as **Dracula, Dirty Old Man** (William Edwards, 1969) and **Sex And The Single Vampire** (Modunk Phreezer, 1970).

LOLITA
Production: USA, 1962
Director: Stanley Kubrick
Category: Sexual Perversion

Nabakov's *Lolita* is the book which gave the world the name now synonymous with "improper" desires towards young girls. **Lolita** was the name chosen by several hardcore porno companies for teenage sex film series in the 70s, and dozens of more overground erotic/exploitation films have used the term in their title, ranging from **Black Lolita** and **Emanuelle And Lolita** to Joe D'Amato's **Anal Perversions Of Lolita**. Kubrick's film is completely tame by comparison, of course, but represents a bold step forward in the screen presentation of "controversial" literature.

MERMAIDS OF TIBURON
Production: USA, 1962/5
Director: John Lamb
Category: Sexy Fantasy

A Diane Webber, a nude model who was *Playboy* magazine's "Playmate of the Month" in May 1955 and in February 1956. The latter feature, photographed by future film director Russ Meyer, included an underwater photo which clearly showed her pubic hair – a *Playboy* first. It was perhaps these scenes of "buxotic" sub-aquatic nudity which prompted John Lamb to cast Webber in his risqué fantasy **Mermaids Of Tiburon**. The film was re-edited in 1965 with added footage of nude actress Gaby Martone and released under the new title **Aqua Sex**. Lamb went on to direct **The Raw Ones** (1965), a voyeuristic documentary on nudism.

MONDO SEXY DI NOTTE
("Sexy Night World")
Production: Italy, 1962
Director: Mino Loy
Category: Sexy Mondo

Loy's first venture in the proto-mondo world of Italian films focusing on the nightclubs, dancing girls and strippers of Europe also gave a name to this type of movie, which became known as the "sexy nocturne". Loy helped drive the genre's focus more and more towards nudity and sex in a series of striptease films that continued with **Notti E Donne Proibite** (1963), **Novanta Notti In Giro Per Il Mondo** (1963), **Supersexy 64** (1963), **Veneri Proibite** (1964), and **Le Mille E Una Donna** (1964). In **Sexy Magico**, a 1963 collaboration with Luigi Scattini, Loy posited similarities between the mysterious sex rites of primitives and urban striptease, feeding into the other main "mondo" theme of deviant atrocities in dark, foreign lands. Loy's films were shot directly in the Crazy Horse or the Sexy Club in Paris, and other hot night spots around the world, and reveal a nocturnal wonderland inhabited by exquisite, exotic, voluptuous naked females with names like Lady Chinchilla, Black Eva, Tartara Wong, Rita Hymalaya, Rafa Temporel, Dodo d'Hamburg, Poupée la Rose, Bonita Super, Véronique, Truda, Lova Moor, Bettina Uranium, Sofia Palladium, and Rosa Fumetto. The sexy nocturne genre exploded during this early 1960s period, giving rise to a deluge of films such as **Sexy** (Renzo Russo, 1962), **Sexy Al Neon** and **Sexy Al Neon 2** (Ettore Fecchi, 1962/1963), **Sexy Ad Alta Tensione** (Oscar De Fina, 1963), **Sexy Che Scotta** (Franco Macchi, 1963), **Sexy Follie, Sexy Nel Mondo** and **Sexy Nudo** (all Roberto Bianchi Montero, 1963), and **Sexy Proibitissimo** (Osvaldo Civirani, Marcello Martinelli, 1963).

NIKUTAI NO ICHIBA
("Flesh Market")
Production: Japan, 1962
Director: Satoru Kobayashi
Category: Sexploitation

Satoru Kobayashi was one of the earliest directors of the Japanese erotic film genre known as *pinku eiga* ("pink film"). This appellation actually arose around 1962/3, of American derivation, and was applied to the low-budget, low-profile "stag" films, with female nudity, being produced by certain independent studios as an early response to the serious fall in audience attendances suddenly being felt by the Japanese studios. Films like **Nikutai No Ichiba** and Koji Seki's **Joyoku No Dokutsu** (1963) are generally regarded as comprising the first wave of the pink genre. Kobayashi went on to direct many more sex films in a long career extending into the 1990s.

PARADISIO
Production: USA, 1962
Director: H. Haile Chace
Category: Nudie-Cutie

SATAN IN HIGH HEELS
Production: USA, 1962
Director: Jerald Intrator
Category: Sexploitation
A noir-styled oddity about a burlesque dancer who rips off her husband and heads to New York to find pleasure in its underworld of sleazy nightclubs. With pneumatic women dressed in leather and even some fleeting nudity to enliven a fairly dull plot. Director Intrator also directed **Orgy At Lil's Place** and later found work shooting hardcore porn inserts for the US release of foreign horror movies.

LA VICE ET LA VERTU

("Vice And Virtue")
Production: France, 1962
Director: Roger Vadim
Category: Sexploitation

At the end of the 1950s, war-films were being made in Europe (including Germany's **Der Letzte Akt**) that have claims to providing the first glimpses of that notorious sub-genre, Nazi sexploitation. The claims of the French film **La Vice Et La Vertu** are strong, and it clearly anticipates Pier Paolo Pasolini's **Salò** (1975) in the way it takes a story by the Marquis de Sade and places it in a WW2 context. Starring Catherine Deneuve and Annie Girardot, Vadim's film is an adaptation of de Sade's *Justine* (1791), the story of two sisters, Justine, who is virtuous, and Juliette, who is vicious. Justine's virtue is punished and Juliette's vice rewarded – here, in the setting of a gothic castle run by the SS. Justine, played by Deneuve, is tortured by an SS officer played by Roger Hossein, and it certainly seems that **La Vice Et La Vertu** is unjustly neglected by those considering the antecedents of the film most widely recognized as the first piece of pure Nazi sexploitation from the US, Bob Cresse's **Love Camp 7**.

INDEX OF MAIN TITLES

À BOUT DE SOUFFLE (1960)	56
LES ABYSSES (1962)	83, 83-84
THE ADVENTURES OF LUCKY PIERRE (1960)	156
AFTER MEIN KAMPF (1961)	71
AI (1962)	168-169
L'AMANTE DEL VAMPIRO (1960)	6, 7
GLI AMORI DI ERCOLE (1960)	98
AMOURS CÉLÈBRES (1961)	161
EL ÁNGEL EXTERMINADOR (1962)	84
THE AVENGERS (1961-69)	133
BACHELOR TOM PEEPING (1962)	169
DIE BANDE DES SCHRECKENS (1960)	57
EL BARÓN DEL TERROR (1962)	41
BEAST OF YUCCA FLATS (1961)	134
BEYOND THE TIME BARRIER (1960)	128
BLAST OF SILENCE (1961)	71
BLAZE STARR GOES NUDIST (1962)	170
DEN BLODIGA TIDEN (1960)	57
BLOODLUST! (1961)	72
LA BRIDE SUR LE COU (1961)	162
THE BRIDES OF DRACULA (1960)	8
LA CABEZA VIVIENTE (1961)	28
CAPE FEAR (1962)	85
LA CAPERUCITA ROJA (1960)	99, 99-100
CAPTAIN CLEGG (1962)	115, 115-116
CARNIVAL OF SOULS (1962)	42
CELLMATES (c.1961)	163
CHELOVEK-AMFIBIYA (1962)	145
LE CIEL ET LA BOUE (1961)	73
CIRCUS OF HORRORS (1960)	9
CITY OF THE DEAD (1960)	10
COLLEGE CONFIDENTIAL (1960)	156, 156-157
LA COMMARE SECCA (1962)	85
COMMON LAW WIFE (1961)	163
LE CONCERTO DE LA PEUR (1962)	170
CONFESSIONS OF AN OPIUM EATER (1962)	86
THE CONNECTION (1961)	74
CREATION OF THE HUMANOIDS (1962)	146
CREATURE FROM THE HAUNTED SEA (1961)	135
CURSE OF THE WEREWOLF (1961)	28, 29
DAI-BOSATSU TOGE (1960)	100, 101
THE DAMNED (1961)	136, 136-137
DAUGHTER OF THE SUN (1962)	171
DAUGHTER OF THE SUN GOD (1962)	116
THE DAY MARS INVADED EARTH (1962)	147
THE DAY THE EARTH CAUGHT FIRE (1961)	137, 137-138
LA DÉNONCIATION (1962)	171
EL DESPOJO (1960)	10-11
THE DEVIL'S MESSENGER (1961)	30
DOCTOR BLOOD'S COFFIN (1960)	11

DOCTOR CRIPPEN (1962)	87
EEGAH (1962)	117
ERCOLE AL CENTRO DELLA TERRA (1961)	107
ERCOLE ALLA CONQUISTA DI ATLANTIDE (1961)	108
EROTICA (1961)	164
EL ESPEJO DE LA BRUJA (1962)	43
ESPIRITISMO (1961)	30
EL ESQUELETO DE LA SEÑORA MORALES (1960)	12
ET MOURIR DE PLAISIR (1960)	13
FANTASMAGORIE (1962)	44
FAUST (1960)	102
FIEND OF DOPE ISLAND (1960)	157
IL FIGLIO DI SPARTACUS (1962)	118
THE FLESH EATERS (1962/64)	148
FLITTERWOCHEN IN DER HÖLLE (1960)	154, 155
FORM MISTRESS (1960)	158
FURYO SHONEN (1961)	75
DAS GEHEIMNIS DER GELBEN NARZISSEN (1961)	75, 75-76
IL GIGANTE DI METROPOLIS (1961)	109, 109-110
IL GLADIATORE INVINCIBILE (1961)	110
IL GOBBO (1960)	12
GORGO (1961)	138
GRITOS EN LA NOCHE (1962)	44, 45
HANAYOME KYUKETSUMA (1960)	14
HAND OF DEATH (1962)	46
HELL IS A CITY (1960)	59
THE HELLFIRE CLUB (1960)	103
HOMICIDAL (1961)	76
HOUSE OF USHER (1960)	15
HOUSE ON BARE MOUNTAIN (1962)	172
HUANG MAO GUIREN (1962)	46-47
THE HYPNOTIC EYE (1960)	60
THE INNOCENTS (1961)	1
INVASION OF THE STAR CREATURES (1962)	149
LA JETÉE (1962)	150
JIGOKU (1960)	16
THE JIVARO SHRINK A HUMAN HEAD (1961)	76
JOURNEY TO THE SEVENTH PLANET (1962)	151
KAIDAN KASANE GA-FUCHI (1960)	16, 17
KAPO (1960)	60, 61
KEY WITNESS (1960)	62
KONGA (1961)	139
KYONETSU NO KISETSU (1960)	154, 55
LEBENSBORN (1961)	165
THE LEECH WOMAN (1960)	18
LA LLORONA (1960)	18
LOLITA (1962)	172
LYCANTHROPUS (1961)	32
MA BARKER'S KILLER BROOD (1960)	62-63, 63
MACISTE ALL'INFERNO (1962)	119
MACISTE CONTRO I MOSTRI (1962)	120
MACISTE CONTRO IL VAMPIRO (1961)	111
MACISTE NELLA VALLE DEI RE (1960)	104
LA MALDICIÓN DE NOSTRADAMUS (1961)	33
MALE AND FEMALE SINCE ADAM AND EVE (1961)	166
LA MANO DE UN HOMBRE MUERTO (1962)	88
MANY WAYS TO SIN (1960)	158
LA MARCA DEL MUERTO (1961)	140
LA MASCHERA DEL DEMONIO (1960)	18, 19
THE MASK (1961)	33
MATKA JOANNA OD ANIOŁÓW (1961)	34
MECHANIZED DEATH (1961)	77
MERMAIDS OF TIBURON (1962/5)	173
MONDO CANE (1962)	89, 89-90
MONDO SEXY DI NOTTE (1962)	174
THE MOST DANGEROUS MAN ALIVE (1961)	141

MOSURA (1961)	142
MR. SARDONICUS (1961)	34, 35
IL MULINO DELLE DONNE DI PIETRO (1960)	20
EL MUNDO DE LOS VAMPIROS (1961)	36
MUNECOS INFERNALES (1961)	36
NAKED – AS NATURE INTENDED (1962)	167, 167-168
NEUTRÓN, EL ENMASCARADO NEGRO (1960)	129
NIGHT OF THE EAGLE (1962)	47
NIGHT TIDE (1961)	37
NIKUTAI NO ICHIBA (1962)	174
NOZ W WODZIE (1962)	90
NUDE ON THE MOON (1960)	159
L'ORRIBILE SEGRETO DEL DR. HICHCOCK (1962)	48
OTOSHIANA (1962)	152
PANIC IN THE YEAR ZERO (1962)	152-153, 153
PARADISIO (1962)	175
THE PHANTOM OF THE OPERA (1962)	49
PHANTOM PLANET (1961)	143
IL PIANETA DEGLI UOMINI SPENTI (1961)	143
THE PICTURE OF DORIAN GRAY (1961)	38
THE PIT (1962)	50
PIT AND THE PENDULUM (1961)	39
PLANETA BUR (1962)	153
THE POLICE AND THE MENTALLY ILL (1960)	63
PORTRAIT OF A MOBSTER (1961)	77, 77-78
THE PREMATURE BURIAL (1962)	50
LE PROCÈS (1962)	92
PSYCHO (1960)	64
DER RACHER (1960)	65
EL RAPTO DE LAS SABINAS (1962)	120
REPTILICUS (1961)	144
THE RISE AND FALL OF LEGS DIAMOND (1960)	66
LA RIVIÈRE DU HIBOU (1962)	51
LA RIVOLTA DEGLI SCHIAVI (1960)	105
DER ROTE RAUSCH (1962)	92
THE RUINED BRUIN (1961)	168
SAFETYBELT FOR SUSIE (1962)	93
SANSONE (1961)	112
SANTO CONTRA LAS MUJERES VAMPIRO (1962)	51, 51-52
SATAN IN HIGH HEELS (1962)	176
DER SCHWEIGENDE STERN (1960)	130
SEDDOK, L'EREDE DI SATANA (1960)	21
SEISHUN ZANKOKU MONOGATARI (1960)	66-68, 67
DIE SELTSAME GRAFIN (1961)	78
SEPPUKU (1962)	121
SHADOW OF THE CAT (1961)	40
SHINOBI NO MONO (1962)	122
THE SINISTER URGE (1961)	79
SPACE-MEN (1960)	131
LA STRAGE DEI VAMPIRI (1962)	52
THE SUBTERRANEANS (1960)	68
TALES OF TERROR (1962)	53
LA TARANTA (1961)	79
TASTE OF FEAR (1961)	79
DIE 1000 AUGEN DES DR, MABUSE (1960)	69
TELL-TALE HEART (1960)	22, 23
DER TEPPICH DES GRAUENS (1962)	93
TERRIFIED (1962)	94
THE TERROR OF THE TONGS (1961)	80
13 GHOSTS (1960)	23
THE TIME MACHINE (1960)	126, 127
TOO HOT TO HANDLE (1960)	70, 71
TORMENTED (1960)	24
DIE TOTEN AUGEN VON LONDON (1961)	81
EIN TOTER HING IM NETZ (1960)	25
IL TRIONFO DI MACISTE (1961)	113

TROPICO DI NOTTE (1961)	168
TRUE GANG MURDERS (1961)	82
THE TWO FACES OF DR. JEKYLL (1960)	26
ULISSE CONTRO ERCOLE (1962)	123
L'ULTIMA PREDA DEL VAMPIRO (1960)	27
URSULA (1961)	40
URSUS (1960)	**106**
URSUS GLADIATORE RIBELLE (1962)	124
EL VAMPIRO SANGRIENTE (1962)	53
VAXDOCKAN (1962)	**125**
LA VENDETTA DI ERCOLE (1960)	96, **97**
LA VÉRITÉ (1960)	**160**
LA VICE ET LA VERTU (1962)	**177**
VILLAGE OF THE DAMNED (1960)	**132**
WEST END JUNGLE (1961)	168
WHATEVER HAPPENED TO BABY JANE? (1962)	95
YOJIMBO (1961)	114
YOURS TRULY, JACK THE RIPPER (1961)	41
ZATOICHI MONOGATARI (1962)	125

ORGY PLUS MASSACRE
SEXY, SCARY & SENSATIONAL CINEMA 1950-1979

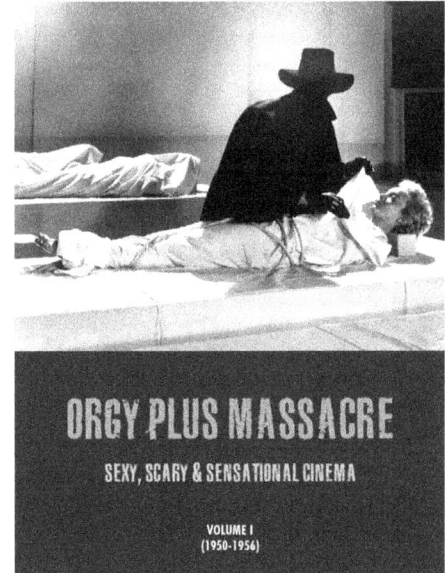

SHADOWS IN A PHANTOM EYE

ATTRACTIONS & ABERRATIONS IN THE MOVING IMAGE 1872-1949

THE COMPLETE 15-VOLUME SERIES

 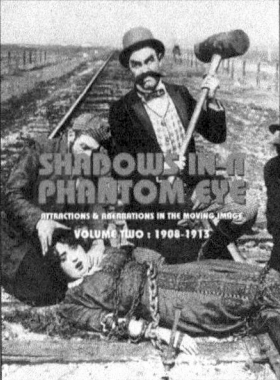  

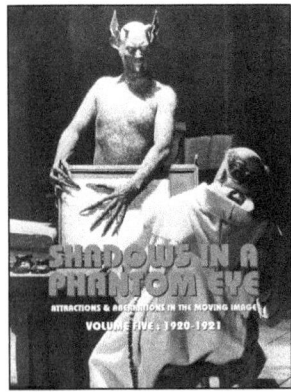   

   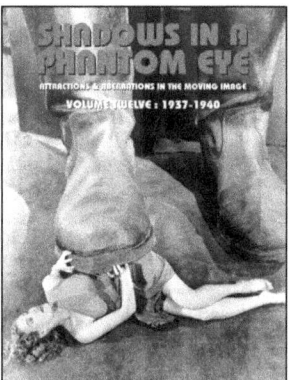